WOMEN RISING

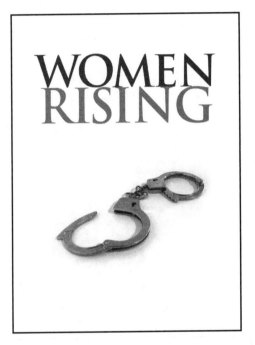

MERRY CHRISTMAS
Compliments of

Prison Fellowship
Canada

WOMEN RISING

How Canadian Women
Are Breaking Free
from Criminal Pasts and
Building a Better Future

ELEANOR CLITHEROE, Editor
FOREWORD BY SHIRLEY CAVANAGH

BASTIAN
BOOKS

Bastian Books
Toronto, Canada
A division of Bastian Publishing Services Ltd.
www.bastianpubserv.com

Distributed by Publishers Group Canada
www.pgcbooks.ca

ISBN 0-978221-2-1

Cataloguing in Publication Data available from Library
and Archives Canada.

Artwork, text layout, and type design by Michaela Miron,
Kinetics Design. Typesetting by Kinetics Design.
www.kdbooks.ca

Printed and bound in Canada by Webcom

To the millions of women
who have been impacted
by crime

CONTENTS

FOREWORD

Shirley Cavanagh

I don't know the women who have contributed to this book, but I am not surprised by their stories of radical transformation in and out of prison. I am married to an ex-prisoner and know first-hand how God changed his life. Jim's pilgrimage began in a darkened cell in the Special Handling Unit of one of Canada's maximum security prisons and has continued right through to the present.

As I write this we have just celebrated twenty years of marriage, and no, it hasn't been like living a life sentence. For the past twenty-three years, Jim has been out of prison. He does return often, not as a repeat offender but to minister to prisoners one-on-one and in chapel groups. He has been speaking to prisoners and the public – including students in high schools – in meetings across Canada, England, Puerto Rico, and the United States. For the past seventeen of those years, he has done so under the auspices of Prison Fellowship Canada.

Jim has bags and bags of letters that he has received over the years from people in many different countries around the world who have read his book about his "release" from prison. These letters share the dramatic effect of his story on their lives. Some of the writers state that they have repented to God in prayer and are growing in their new-found faith.

It is my prayer that the dramatic, redemptive stories that follow in this book will encourage you to take a look at your own attitudes toward those in trouble with the law – and to give God a chance to work in your life.

SHIRLEY CAVANAGH
Kingston, Ontario

PREFACE

THE genesis of this book was a lunch hosted
by Shirley Kiervin. On a beautiful August day in
Oakville, Ontario, fifty women gathered in her
backyard to hear the stories of women whose lives
had been affected by brokenness and crime. And
they also joined her in contributing financially to
the preparation of this book – a collection of such
stories. Our heartfelt thanks go out to everyone at
that meeting. All of the profits from the book's sales
will go directly into the work of Prison Fellowship
Canada.

This book was written to raise the concerns
of women who are impacted by crime, whether
as offenders, ex-offenders, or family members.
Women's needs, fears, and aspirations are often

not addressed as they should be, and women need to be strong and support each other in raising their voices.

Prison Fellowship Canada is a faith-based organization that believes three things about people: first, created by God, we are good; second we all make mistakes and separate ourselves from God; and third, with help and courage, we can transform our lives. The focus of PFC volunteers across this country is to walk beside people broken by crime – in the prisons and in the community.

Our thanks to everyone who helped make this book possible, both the women who have had the courage to tell their stories and those who supported them in the telling. Thank you, Shirley and Jack Kiervin, for your confidence; Judith Laus, for your unfailing love for the mission; and Don Bastian, for seeing the power of this book from our first meeting.

ELEANOR CLITHEROE

Introduction

Eleanor Clitheroe

WE'VE all been there, sitting in front of our televisions grousing over the soft treatment of Canadian criminals. *Why can't the justice system give them what they deserve? Why can't we just put them in jail and throw away the key? We'd be better off, and so would they: at least they would only have each other to hurt.*

Some of us do come down a few steps from our pulpits when the subject is women committing crime, since the images in our minds, as we launch our sermons, are mostly male. But we still wish the problem could just be handled once and for all, leaving us in peace and safety.

As you are about to find out through reading the stories in this book of women involved in the prison system – a current prisoner, several ex-offenders, and two daughters of ex-offenders – the situation is not nearly as simple as that. Most women who commit crime really are influenced by their upbringing and circumstances, and, often, their fight for survival. And the prison system really does take raw recruits and turn them into career criminals. And those career criminals really do recommit crimes and get a pass back to jail.

However, it doesn't have to be this way. Across this country, through the support of various church and community organizations, Canada's women prisoners are breaking free from lives of hopelessness and suffering and are being restored to their families and friends and neighbourhoods and society at large.

I am blessed to be part of one such group. I am executive director of Prison Fellowship Canada, which partners with local churches across the country to minister to those whom society often scorns or at least neglects: prisoners, ex-prisoners, and their families. Prison Fellowship reaches out to them both as an act of service to Jesus Christ and as a contribution to restoring peace to our communities endangered by crime. We operate on the assumption, and experience, that the best way to transform our communities is to transform the people within those communities. We are one of many such ministry and outreach programs that help to keep a candle lit in the windows of the homes of women prisoners until they can achieve reinstatement in their homes and in society.

As you read the stories by such women, you may find yourself turning away from the television screen that has you in full cry against the injustices of the justice system to see, feel, and care about what's really going on out there.

In this book you will read the dramatic stories of:

- ⊘ **Vivienne Nash**, who as a young single mother built her identity and a good income in the world of drug smuggling – before discovering real identity and wealth through God.

- ⊘ **Dewey**, who as a teenager entered a marriage that ended in turmoil, but went on to see her life and family restored.

- ⊘ **Janie Nadeau**, who found God to be more than an adequate replacement for the spoon, the needle, and the drugs in her search for a place to belong.

∞ **Carol Andrews**, who as a teenager fell into destructive relationships with men. Sent to prison after the death of one of her lovers, she finally found God and, in him, the skills, the courage, and the will to start life over again.

∞ **Stacey-Ann Bucknor**, the daughter of an offender, whose lost decade was turned into the life she always longed for.

∞ **Christina**, who witnessed the fight that led to her father's death and her mother's imprisonment – and went into full battle mode to protect her brothers and keep her family together.

∞ **Stephanie Martin**, still in prison at publication time, weaning herself from the alcohol and drug addictions that fuelled her "commute" between the street and prison most of her young life.

The book closes with my own story of how I came to be involved in this challenging and fulfilling ministry. My hope, and that of everyone at Prison Fellowship Canada, is that *Women Rising* will inspire you to become part of the solution, not the problem – that you will join in this great effort to restore Canadian women prisoners to their homes and society.

Vivienne Nash

THREE WARNINGS
AND A SECOND CHANCE

"What will be in the package?" I asked him.

"A kilo of cocaine," he said, looking into my eyes to gage my reaction.

I'm amazed that I agreed to do it. I didn't even think about the danger I could be getting myself into, or what it would cost me if I got caught. I needed the money so badly, I couldn't say no. Besides, I liked this guy. I would have done anything for him.

I spent my earliest years living a sheltered life with my aunt and a cousin in downtown Kingston, Jamaica. My aunt was taking care of me because my mother had moved to Toronto when I was five. She went there to be a nanny for a family she had worked for in Kingston.

In 1974, when I was eight, I was packed up and put on an Air Canada flight to Toronto. I was watched over by one of the stewardesses during the trip, but I was nervous. This was my first airplane flight, and I was about to be reunited with my mother, whom I had not seen for several years. I was excited, too. As far as I was concerned, I needed my mother's care and her care alone. It wasn't that my aunt was doing a poor job. It was just that nothing beats the care of a mother.

I was the youngest of three children, all of us

now living with a single mom in a four-storey apartment building in the Keele and Wilson area of Toronto. Mom always loved me dearly, but I missed the presence of a father in the home. My two brothers were the closest thing to a father figure I had, but they both got married early, leaving home when I was sixteen.

I always imagined that when I grew up I would make new friends and make a better life for myself. I had a lot of issues with my weight. I wished I could be like the other girls. I was always anxious for people to like me. I believed I would never know what it was like to be attractive.

As a teenager I heard my friends talk about their relationships and all the good things that came with them. And there I was – I didn't even know what it was like to have a boyfriend.

One night, when I was sixteen, I went to a house party with a group of friends. I was introduced to an attractive man four years older than me. He was about six feet tall, dark in complexion, medium of build, a high-school student who was working downtown as a chef in a restaurant at Eaton Centre. At first I didn't feel anything at all for him, but the fact that he seemed interested in me was good enough for me. He and I started dating.

I knew he came from a good home. My friends

knew him, and I took their word that he was a nice guy. He treated me well, and my mother liked him a lot.

When I met him I was the only one in my group of girlfriends who was still a virgin. My girlfriends were always talking about sex and how much they enjoyed it, and I felt so left out. As my boyfriend and I got more involved, I started skipping school to be with him. (I wasn't allowed to be out late at night because I was so young.) It was on one of those days on the lam from school that I lost my virginity.

At around that time, my best friend found out she was pregnant. Her mother called my mother about it. I overheard my mother say, "I don't know what I would do if it was my daughter." Well, she got to find out, because within two months it *was* her daughter. My boyfriend and I had been together for about six months when I discovered I was pregnant. I thought I was going to lose my mind – not that it mattered that much: I was pretty sure my mother was going to kill me anyway.

When my doctor called me into his office for the results, I was so scared, I took a friend with me. When he told me I was pregnant, I felt I was going to faint. The doctor told me I had a week to think about what I wanted to do – whether to carry the baby or abort it. Even though I was only seventeen, abortion was not an option for me. No matter what, I wanted to keep this child.

On October 20, 1983, I gave birth to a beautiful baby girl, Stacey, and she has been the joy of my life ever since.

After my daughter's birth, my boyfriend asked me to marry him because he wanted us to raise her together. In December of the same year, we got engaged.

That's when things started to change for us. His family liked me fine as a girlfriend, but as a wife, I just wasn't good enough. His mother disliked me. He was the last of nine children, and she was jealous of the attention he was giving me. The pressure caused our relationship to go downhill. We got into more and more fights.

We had opened a bank account before things started going bad between us. Now, his mother began advising him to take his share of the money out of the account. He had been in this situation before, and his girlfriend had drained the account and run. His mother kept reminding him of this sad tale, predicting I would do the same thing.

One day he told me he wanted to close the account and split the money so he could get his mother off his back. But I listened to my mother's advice that I should let him keep the money and get out of the relationship.

When the relationship did come to an end, my daughter was two years old and I was left to fend for myself. It's true I was living at home with my mother, but she wasn't making enough money to feed herself and two other mouths. She did what she could, but beyond that I was on my own.

In my daughter's earliest years I was a stay-at-home welfare mom. Things just kept getting worse, financially. I decided that no matter what it took, I was going to find a way to take care of my daughter. I sometimes asked my ex-fiancé for money for her, but he always said he had nothing to give.

The years went by. At times I was working two jobs to make ends meet. For a time I was working a particularly crazy schedule. I checked bags at the airport from 1 p.m. to 9 p.m. and then worked in the Howard Johnson's, also at the airport, from 10 p.m. to 5 a.m. Even so, it wasn't enough. I was getting fed up with my situation. My daughter was starting school and needed new clothes. The demands were becoming unbearable. All I wanted was some quick cash.

To ease the stress, I started clubbing with my friends. Because I lived with my mother, I didn't really have to worry about finding or paying a baby-sitter, so I went out almost every weekend, mainly to the Jane and Finch area to the west of our neighbourhood. I would make sure my daughter was safely tucked into bed. Then off I would go into the night.

On one of these occasions I noticed a new guy at the club talking to one of my friends. He was very good looking. He came over to me and introduced himself as Michael. He bought drinks for me and all my friends. I could see that he had a lot of money. I hoped to see him again.

The next weekend my friends and I went to the club, and Michael was there again.

"I really like that guy," I said to my friend.

"Why don't you tell him?" she said with a smile.

Not in this lifetime would he ever like me, I remember thinking. I was not his type. For sure he would have a girlfriend.

But Michael came over to our table and we began to talk.

Not long into our conversation, he popped the question: "Do you want to make some money?"

"How much money are you talking about?" I replied.

"Three thousand dollars."

I couldn't believe my ears. This could change everything. I would be able to buy new clothes for Stacey and me. I could enroll her in a better school. I could pay some bills off and stop dreading the end of every month.

"Sure," I said. "Why not?"

Michael agreed to meet me a little while later to talk about it. I felt good knowing that we would be together again.

He called me within a few weeks. Over coffee at a shop across from my apartment, he asked me if I was still interested in making some money, and I told him yes.

All I had to do, Michael said, was fly to New York City, meet some friends of his in the Bronx, and then fly back with a package they would give me for him.

"What will be in the package?" I asked him.

"A kilo of cocaine," he said, looking into my eyes to gage my reaction.

I'm amazed that I agreed to do it. I didn't even think about the danger I could be getting myself into, or what it would cost me if I got caught. I needed the money so badly, I couldn't say no. Besides, I liked this guy. I would have done anything for him.

And that's how I started trafficking drugs. I was very nervous on that first run, but as I made repeated trips to New York and various cities in the Caribbean, it became like a job for me. I would get up early in the morning, drive to the airport, board a flight to my destination, and then head back home. Just another day at the office.

I was working for a courier company at the time, which gave me the perfect cover. I posed as being on business for that company, and everything worked out fine.

I became very good at what I did. Over the years I made new friends who were working in the same circles. As for Michael, he didn't matter that much to me anymore – I was making plenty of money and meeting lots of other guys. I acquired a reputation in this crowd for being a carrier everyone could count on to get their stuff to them. Once, just a few weeks after a major bust, everyone was afraid to carry anything. But I still came through for Michael.

Becoming a well-known trafficker did wonders for my self-esteem. I was in high demand. I started getting phone calls from all over. I had developed a unique and useful talent, and everyone knew it.

Furthermore, I was in control of things for the first time in my life. My daughter and I had our own apartment, not far from where my mother lived. I could buy my daughter anything she wanted. I could have whatever I wanted. I had more friends now than ever before. I treated people well, and they respected me. I was working internationally for big money. I had connections all over Canada, the United States, and the Caribbean. Things were going so well, I was even thinking of starting my own operation.

And I was getting to the stage where I wouldn't have to carry drugs myself. In fact, on a job coming up, I was to fly down to Jamaica to meet two girls and lead them through the steps of flying back with the drugs. I was now able to work as a recruiter and simply assist those who would be carrying.

Before and during that trip to Jamaica, I received three clear warnings not to proceed with the operation.

The morning before I left, my daughter said, "Mom, I had a dream that you were in jail." I didn't pay any attention to her.

Amazingly, my mother – who did not know the true nature of my activities – called me the same morning and told me she had dreamed that I had gotten into trouble at an airport. Again, I ignored what I was hearing.

I lit down at the Kingston airport on a beautiful and very hot March evening and went straight to my hotel, which was about twenty minutes away. I met with my associates there, who had arrived the day before. We went over the plans, and I was satisfied that everything was in place. Just before the evening ended, I was asked by one of the leaders of the group to carry two bags myself in this operation. I consented to the change in plans but vowed that this would be the last time. I was getting tired of taking the risk and was ready to move up a level in the business.

Our flight was leaving the next morning, so I went to bed early in order to be focused the next day.

At daybreak I called a cab and loaded my bags into the trunk. For some reason, though, I couldn't get into the cab. I realize now that I was receiving warning number three, whether from my own instincts or a higher power, I didn't know at the time. I nearly listened to this one. I left the cab waiting and ran back to the hotel room to talk to my friend, who had been staying in the room with me.

"Something's wrong," I told him. "I don't know

what it is. I don't think we should go ahead with this."

"Don't worry yourself about it. Everything will be fine," he assured me.

I went back to the cab, but the same uneasy feeling came over me. I went to talk to my friend again, and he settled me down again. After that I was able to proceed to the airport.

Once there I met up with the others. Everything was set up perfectly. The check-in process always went smoothly because we had connections with people inside airport security. We checked our bags and met again in the waiting area. Our flight was on time. Within twenty-five minutes the announcement came that it was time to board the plane, and we proceeded toward the gate.

The drugs were in our carry-on luggage. There were three others beside me: the two carriers I was supervising, and one of the leaders of the group. I was the first in line. There was nothing to worry about. The security staff at this gate worked with us. One of them had even been part of the meeting the night before at the hotel. But as I approached the gate, my long streak of luck finally ran out. A young woman I'd never seen before called me over to check my bag. She promptly found the thirty-four pounds of marijuana I was carrying.

At the time of my arrest I was not saved. I didn't realize that it was the Lord speaking to me just a few hours earlier at the hotel. I also did not recognize his voice in the dreams of my daughter and mother.

Life in the Caribbean may be slow-paced, but justice can be very swift. There would be no bail for me, and no court appeals to forestall the inevitable, either. I was arrested and charged, and then convicted and sent straight to jail in Kingston and do not pass go. My sentence was for sixteen months.

The worst jail in Canada would be like Club Med in comparison with the rathole they put me in. There were twenty women in each cell. We slept on cardboard mattresses placed on low metal frames.

When I was arrested, everyone turned their back on me, including the guys I was working for. I didn't give any of their names to the authorities when I was taken to court. I took the blame and did the time all by myself.

As awful as the sixteen months in prison were – and being cut off from my daughter was the worst part of it – I did have plenty of time to think about where I wanted to go with my life.

I met a wonderful lady who was serving a life sentence. She had given her heart to the Lord while inside. She started talking to me about how she had come to know the Lord. I was very drawn to her and spent a lot of time listening to her. I often wrote out the Christian songs that she sang to me and the Bible verses she quoted.

On the Christmas morning of my time there a Salvation Army group came into the institution to play in the Christmas service. I don't know whether it was because I wanted to hear a word from God or just get out of my cell for a while, but I was excited to go to chapel.

As my sentence came to an end, I was afraid to go back out into the real world. I knew I was going to face a lot of hardship and temptation. Before my arrest, I had become accustomed to having a lot of money – now, I would have nothing but the clothes on my back.

I wish I could tell you I stayed on the straight and narrow once I got back to Canada, but my prediction was true: I did face hardship and I did face temptation and I did get into trouble again. However, through my spiritual reflexes may have been a bit slow, the ministry of that woman in the Kingston prison was beginning to have its effect on me.

Stacey was twelve by this time, and I was worried about what she would become – after all, her mother was not exactly a sterling role model. I didn't want her to make the same mistakes I had made. I also didn't want to bring shame into her life. I knew I had to change my life for her sake. That was my turning point: when I stopped thinking about me and started thinking about her.

I enrolled in a community college, training as a medical and dental assistant. I also started attending a Pentecostal church and enjoyed the fellowship of the people there. I could tell I was changing because I was losing my appetite for clubbing and living dangerously.

Nothing could have prepared me, however, for the transformation I was about to experience.

I had kept up with some of my old friends and still went out with them to the club now and then. One Saturday I met some of them there. As we stood at the bar, I felt a sensation of heat come over my body. The club was full of people, but that wasn't the heat that I was feeling: it was something I'd never experienced before, a warmth that was coming out from under my skin.

I told my friend I was going outside for a minute.

I sat in my car and the tears poured out of me like a rushing river. I began repenting of all the wrong things I had done – and all of them seemed to parade past me. I asked God to forgive me for every time I had brought marijuana or cocaine into this country. For every time someone's child had become hooked on one of these drugs because of me. For every time I had let my own child down.

∞

Something was happening to me, but I didn't know the extent of it yet.

I started going to church more regularly and even attended Bible studies. I told my pastor I had already accepted the Lord as my Saviour but now needed to be baptized.

Two years into my new life, the Spirit of the Lord impressed upon my heart that I should become an evangelist and help people avoid – or recover from – a life like mine. I could not believe that God would place such a desire within me, an ex-inmate. Nevertheless, he chose me for this ministry. During my time as a prisoner, I thought it possible I would end up returning to jail – but as a repeat offender, not because I had a word of hope to deliver. But of course it all makes sense. I was highly qualified for this work: I knew what it was like on the inside. I knew what it was like on the outside after having been on the inside. I had a testimony that fit the ministry I was being called to do.

I have been saved now for eight years. Staying on the straight and narrow was very difficult in the beginning, but God was right there beside me every step of the way.

I work for Prison Fellowship now, speaking about prison ministries to church groups and talking to prisoners and ex-prisoners right across the country. I came to the attention of Prison Fellowship because of the work I was doing in my local church, helping people pray for those in jail and support them financially.

God has blessed me with the ability to connect with people and make them feel at ease. I used to apply those skills to get through airports with my dangerous cargo. I am applying them to transport precious cargo now.

Best of all, after changing the course of my life, I was better able to instruct my daughter in the way to go and – glory be to God – she has grown up to be a wonderful young lady. And as for my poor long-suffering mother, at last she is able to enjoy and respect her daughter.

My desire is to go back and spread the gospel to

every country where I once picked up drugs. I want to let people know that no matter who they are or what they have done, God will give them a second chance, too.

Dewey

WHITE LACE,
BROKEN PROMISES

*I would go to work and
stare into space until my
manager told me I might
as well just go home.
But going home early
wasn't an option. It
would mean sipping tea
with my mother-in-law,
pretending everything
was fine. She didn't
know – and didn't want
to know – what was
really going on between
her son and me.*

FOR most of my life I felt guilty that I wasn't grateful for how my life was turning out. I was in a successful career as a social worker and had three great children: a girl and two boys. And yet I was always haunted by the feeling that I never really *belonged* in my own life. In the end, it took years of domestic hardship, the death of my husband, a stay in prison, and the infinite mercy of God to finally show me I had been in denial about my past all along.

I was born in London, England, in 1961. My father, who had moved to the United Kingdom from the Caribbean, was training to be a welder. My mother, who was a seamstress or a dressmaker, I believe, had met him in Sheffield, Yorkshire, where they were married shortly after.

I have only a few sketchy memories of our flat in the southwestern part of London. It was the second floor of a house, as I recall. My earliest memories are of visits by my dad's four brothers – they were a lively and fun-loving bunch and definitely left an impression on me. But that's about it.

I also remember, very clearly, the day my world fell apart. I was only six years old. The day started when my mother and I boarded a train in Sheffield bound for London. We had been in Sheffield with her family. Once we reached London, we took the tube to our home. We climbed up the stairs to our flat. To my surprise, I was unceremoniously handed over to my father with my mother making as if to leave. The three of us were standing uncomfortably in the kitchen where Dad had laid out a full English breakfast for this occasion. My mom refused his invitation to stay and eat with us. She just started crying and ran down the stairs and onto the street and out of our lives. I never saw her again.

No one told me what was going on. I had been led to believe that Mom was coming back to London to be with Dad and me. No one offered any explanation why their relationship had ended. Both of them did everything they could to protect me from the truth: my father by not saying a word to me about it, and my mother by not saying a word to me about anything. She removed herself completely from our lives.

My dad believed he could provide for all my needs physically, mentally, and emotionally. That's what he thought he was doing when he kept my past a secret. That's what he thought he was doing when he shut me down if I ever uttered anything on the topic of loss. My mother's very existence was simply off limits.

Recently, with my father's passing, I came across his photos from this time in my life. One of them is eerily prophetic. In the photo I am not yet a year old. My father is seated and I am on his lap. My mother is standing beside us.

For a few months after that fateful morning, it was just Dad and me. Then he entered into another relationship. From that union I would be joined, when I was eight years old, by a stepsister. By this time we had moved to Toronto, where Dad took up a job as a welder until an accident – he got metal in his eye – forced him to change professions. He took some courses at George Brown College and became a jeweler, eventually owning his own jewelry store.

On the outside, our family seemed normal. Maybe even happy. But in my heart I knew things were not right. No one can replace a biological mother – it's simply impossible to make up for such a loss.

Not only was I not allowed closure over my mother's exit from our family, I was also not allowed closure over her exit from this planet. At the young age of forty-two, when I was twenty, she went into a diabetic coma, dying soon after. I did not attend her funeral in Sheffield. Dad was nothing if not consistent: he thought it would be too painful for me.

My memories of the time before my mother left us are happy ones. At least these were the memories Dad wanted me to hold on to. We were raised to accept things as they were and not ask questions. As I reached my teenage years, I retreated to my room when things became difficult. I tuned out anything that was stressful. It was the only way I could cope.

My stepsister left home to study law at a school in Pennsylvania and went on to become a successful lawyer in Atlanta. When I left home, eight years before her, at age nineteen, I couldn't wait to get married and have children – to make a life for myself that was full of the love I had been missing.

Let me take you back to the late 1970s, which is when I met my Prince Charming. I was just starting high school, in Toronto, and he was in his final year at the same school. He was four years older than I was. He was tall, dark, and handsome, and he had a car. What more could a girl ask for?

I'd been taught, growing up Roman Catholic, that marriage was the road to happiness. A lifetime of marital bliss – "until death do us part" – was my constant dream.

After four years of dating – and just as I was into my first year of college in Toronto – we got married. I became pregnant soon after. Seemingly overnight I was a wife, the mother of a beautiful girl, and a very serious student in a social work program. I spent my days with diapers in one hand and books in the other. Perhaps my social worker's desire to save the world gave me the energy to hold my world together.

In hindsight I can see there were warning signs not to get in the matrimonial way with this man. The first was that I was just nineteen when we decided to get married. We had to obtain special permission from the Catholic Church. At the time – sensibly, I now realize – the church didn't ordinarily marry anyone under the age of twenty-one without parental permission.

WOMEN RISING

The second was my husband's lack of ambition. He was barely able to earn his grade twelve diploma and had no interest in continuing his education after that. It became increasingly clear that he was not taking his responsibilities seriously. After graduation he was off the job more than he was on it. He left one job suddenly, when I was eight months' pregnant with Baby Number Two, a boy. This self-imposed layoff would last six years.

During this time our dream home in Mississauga became our nightmare home. After three years there, we were having trouble making the mortgage payments. We had to move back to Toronto to live with my husband's mother. Meanwhile, he just kept nursing dreams of starting his own business, never taking even one baby step toward making it happen.

When I graduated from college, I was lucky enough to find a job in my field right away. Over the years I was able to support my family even when my husband couldn't or wouldn't. In fact, I have been employed by the same organization for over twenty years now.

True to my upbringing, anytime I started to question my husband's behaviour, I shut my thoughts down. I would remind myself that his upbringing was even tougher than mine. His father had come to Canada as a refugee from a Communist country and had struggled to make a life here. He had beaten my husband frequently throughout his childhood while his wife stood by. Aware of my husband's hurt feelings, I didn't dare disagree with anything he said or wanted. Even constructive criticism would have been too much. I was practically a genius at putting up and shutting up, even, or maybe especially, during the rockiest years of our marriage. I kept my focus on the children and kept myself busy at work and in my community.

Where I came from, you didn't air your dirty laundry in public. I never complained. I always put my husband's needs before mine. I even put him on a pedestal. I believed in my heart and soul that my job as a dutiful and submissive wife was to make my husband look good, to support him regardless of how messed up he was. My PR skills must have been pretty good: I had my friends and relatives believing my glowing reports of what a doting husband and father he was.

After our third child, a son, was diagnosed with autism, things really started to fall apart between us. At first my husband was in denial. He referred to Nicky's diagnosis as a "little problem." But over time it became clear even to him just how big this little problem was. I don't doubt for a second that my husband loved Nicky; it was just that he just didn't know how to deal with him. He would get upset with him and panic. Sometimes he called me at work because he couldn't figure out how to take care of him; sometimes he got so angry he would break things around the house. He just couldn't handle stress.

Meanwhile, I was scrambling to get Nicky all the support he needed and was entitled to. I read everything I could get my hands on about his condition and joined support groups. But Nicky's progress was slow. It was very tiring trying to communicate with him and teach him new skills. My husband always put on a brave face, but inside he wasn't coping. There was more and more fighting in the house. Even so, the more stressed out he became, the more I made sure I was in agreement with him, even when I knew he was wrong. This was the only way I knew how to behave in a relationship.

In the fall of 2000, I figured out that my husband was having an affair with a woman from the store where he was working. One day I innocently called him at work and his supervisor told me he'd gone home ill several hours before. Later that day my husband left me a message saying he didn't need me to pick him up at work – he'd made other arrangements to get home.

My husband became reclusive and withdrawn with me and the kids. He would come home and go straight to bed. When he was awake, he was at work or with his girlfriend.

I visited my family priest for advice. The next day my husband agreed to come with me to see the priest, but insisted on talking to him alone. I went to confession in connection with this appointment, but my husband refused to do so. The priest whispered to me, "I cannot force him to go to confession. I can only pray for your marriage."

The next day my husband didn't come home from work. He stayed out all night and didn't call me till the next morning. When he arrived home that evening, we got into an awful fight. I pleaded with him to see a marriage counsellor with me. I actually got him to do so, but he lasted only one session, during which he told me he didn't want to be married to me anymore. Of course, he showed his trademark lack of responsibility in this matter, too: he kept putting off applying for a divorce or making any plans to leave home.

By this time I had fallen into a deep depression.

I had lost a sense of who I was. I struggled with the fact that I couldn't fix my marriage, that I couldn't make things right, no matter how desperately I tried. I was barely functioning. I would go to work and stare into space until my manager told me I might as well just go home. But going home early wasn't an option. It would mean sipping tea with my mother-in-law, pretending everything was fine. She didn't know – and didn't want to know – what was really going on between her son and me. Staunch Catholics that she and I were, that was a conversation we simply could not have.

Instead I would cruise along the streets of the city in the big beige Audi we had bought at an auction. It's a wonder I was able to keep the car on the road as I cried, prayed, and agonized over my family and our future.

I did get counselling for myself – my husband again refused to come with me – but I still wasn't ready to admit our marriage was past saving.

I withdrew further and further from society. I began to lose weight and became ill emotionally, mentally, and physically.

I had just enough awareness to know I could not function in this nerve-wracking situation. I begged my husband to leave, or to let me leave. By this time we were finally in agreement that the marriage was over, but that didn't mean we were rid of each other. I no longer wanted to live with him in the same house, but he wasn't going anywhere fast. What was I to do?

I contacted a real estate agent, who showed me a few lower-end homes, but I couldn't come up with the down payment for any of them.

After almost three months of this agony, as the year was drawing to a close, I finally came out of denial. I listened to my friends' advice and went to see a divorce lawyer, which was a major step for a devout Catholic. I told the lawyer I had to get out of my home. She advised me that if I did so, it should only be for a short period of time. It might be difficult to get custody of my children if I was the one to leave, she told me. Besides, getting back into the house could be a problem, since it was owned by my mother-in-law.

I just couldn't keep the charade going any longer. I decided that I needed some time alone. My sister was coming up from Atlanta for a visit. I talked to her about returning with her to her home for a short time after the holidays. That would allow me to distance myself from the excruciating pain I was experiencing. My husband objected vigorously to the prospect of being left at home with the kids, but I was determined to go.

It was about a week before Christmas when the end finally came.

My poor mother-in-law, God bless her, was baking, cooking, and wrapping presents, unaware of the heartache that lay ahead.

Things were getting crazier and crazier. My husband's mistress was shameless, flaunting their affair in my face. She called him late at night. My neighbours saw her waiting outside our house in her car in the mornings to pick him up for work. The two of them were now scheduling their days off together. I had had enough. The decision was clear: I had to start divorce proceedings and get out of the house. It was obvious that he wasn't going to leave.

The decision to leave my kids for a while, especially with one of them being a special-needs child, was the hardest I had ever had to make. My kids were, and are, my whole life. But I was turning into a zombie. I needed some time to figure out where my life was going, now that this twenty-four-year episode was coming to an end. I thought my trip to the U.S. with my sister would be my saving grace.

My husband and I agreed to meet at a restaurant to discuss who would take care of the kids, the details of our finances, and the day-to-day matters he would need to attend to after I left. He was apologetic the whole time. He cried like a baby and kept on saying that he didn't want to hurt me – he just wanted me to be his best friend. I was cold and detached and did not shed a tear. It was as if I was sitting there with a total stranger.

We agreed that the day after Christmas I would be leaving on the plane with my sister to her home in Atlanta. After we finished talking, he told me he needed some time alone to deal with the reality that our relationship was over. He dropped me off at the house and drove off, presumably to see you-know-who.

For the first time in a very long time I could actually hear myself breathing. I was beginning to feel I actually had some control over my life again.

Late that night, at about 2 a.m., after I had gone to bed, I heard the front door open and close. It was my husband. He started yelling at me before he reached the top of the stairs. In his rage he told me I was a bad mother. He blamed me for my son's illness. I got out of bed to confront him, and the next hour featured name-calling, yelling, the hurling back and forth of accusations, and some pushing and shoving.

"You aren't the one who's leaving," he yelled. "I am."

"And who would be behind that decision?" I yelled back. "Did you come up with that or was it your girlfriend?"

I knew she was the one behind this change in tactics. She didn't want to be saddled with an autistic child. She didn't even have custody of her own three children.

Our argument turned into a terrible physical battle. We fought to get control of a knife, and the next thing I remember the police were barging into the room. My mother-in-law, awakened by all the noise, had finally decided she'd better call them. My husband and I were both covered in blood. I was blind in my right eye from a knife wound. I also had slash wounds to both of my hands. He was bleeding profusely from his chest and the base of his neck.

I was arrested by the police, charged with attempted murder, and escorted in handcuffs to the emergency room of the hospital nearby.

All the time that the doctors and nurses were attending to my wounds and trying to get me to calm down, I assumed that my husband was in the bed next to mine. I screamed out in disbelief when the officer informed me that he had bled out and died on the way to the hospital.

∞

I'd like to say I was preoccupied with his death, and my part in it, in the days that followed. I did feel terrible about it, and I did feel guilty. However, the next six weeks – the amount of time I was in the detention centre while my lawyer was arranging bail for me – are hard for me to remember.

I do recall learning that my charge had been "upgraded" from manslaughter to murder. I remember the anxiety I felt each evening as I stood in line to use the phone for a quick conversation with my dad and children. If you didn't get your turn before 9 p.m., you wouldn't get to make your call. It was so painful when that happened – I had no way to reassure my loved ones that I hadn't forgotten them.

The events that led to my situation, including the loss of my husband, and in such a terrible way, percolated through my consciousness. The separation from my three children was unbearable. But mostly I was in a blur. There were medical reasons for that. I was drugged practically the whole time, to control the pain from my wounds. I have vague memories of trips to specialists to determine what was going to happen to my eye.

⌒⌒

After those six weeks I was granted bail by the judge, based on my lawyer's submission. I finally got the chance to go home and see my kids – to Dad's home, that is: he had swooped in and taken the children from my mother-in-law's house as soon as he learned what had happened.

I also visited an eye doctor and did what I had to do to have a prosthetic eye put in.

Four months into my time on bail I decided to return to work in order to achieve some sense of normalcy. The transition back to work was very difficult, but I was able to put up with the spectators and embrace the well-wishers.

During this time I received a lot of support from friends, family, and co-workers, including the senior management at work. (The general manager had written a letter that helped me obtain release on bail.) Throughout my initial incarceration and my three years on bail, I attended spiritual courses. I also went into therapy as a condition of bail. I learned a lot about who I was. After a lifetime of avoiding truths about my life, I finally got to know *me* intimately. I began to see that the issues you try to run away from do eventually catch up to you – that the only way to know true strength and inner peace is by acknowledging the grief and loss in your life.

During those years of waiting, I went to an evangelical Protestant church that my father had been attending, in spite of his Catholic upbringing. He told me that joining a Bible study with other women there would help me, and he was right. These women became very close to me, and even came to see me when I was eventually in prison.

After three years, I ran out of money and took a plea bargain rather than going through a trial. I was sentenced to five years in jail.

In some ways it would have been easier to have gone straight to jail after that terrible night. It was heart wrenching to know, each and every day of my three years on bail, that in all likelihood separation from my family lay ahead of me.

But Dad was right. The three years of spiritual nurture ended up giving me the strength to get through the loss of freedom that I had to endure.

The prison I was sent to, in Ontario, was nothing like what I imagined. It was actually a village of homes. Inmates had quite a bit of freedom to move around the grounds. We even got to see our kids on the weekends for extended periods. Still, it was prison. We had no choice but to stay there and pay for what we had done. I kept myself busy by taking college courses. And being an unrepentant social worker, I ended up counselling other inmates through their difficulties.

Eventually I became secretary to the prison chaplain. That's how I came to know about Prison Fellowship and the work they do with inmates and their kids: making sure the latter receive birthday gifts and Christmas gifts, counselling the former, doing what they could to hold families together until Mom comes home.

There is a misconception in society that bad things happen to bad people and that if you're in prison it's probably because you deserve to be. The truth is, many people in jail really are victims of their circumstances. Many are good people who made bad choices. Somewhere along the line they lost their way, leading to tragedy.

After fourteen months in jail, I was released on day parole. I decided to keep on helping women in situations similar to mine. Six months after that, I was released outright. I am now back at work full time. I have custody of all three of my beautiful children, and all of us are happily settled into a new house that I was able to buy while on parole.

God is a God of second chances. Nothing is

impossible for him. Things are done in his time, not ours. We need to trust him and wait on him, believing by faith that we can make it in spite of the worst of odds.

I am a living witness that it is possible to rise above one's circumstances and acts and be free.

Pass it on: There is life after prison.

Janie Nadeau

A PLACE
TO BELONG

I remember that night
so clearly. The beat-up
duplex, the people there
passing a needle around.
When it was my turn,
I stuck out my arm,
closed my eyes, and
felt the most wonderful
calmness flow into me.
I quickly grew
dependent on that
feeling to make me
feel safe inside.

I was born into a family that was not ready to be one. My mother got pregnant at age sixteen, and in those days when you got pregnant you got married. I was born into this family in 1960, in Edmonton, Alberta, where we lived until I was two. Some of my earliest memories are not pleasant ones – for example, of the times I had to flee to a motel with my mother until things calmed down back at home.

My mother tried to be a good mom. She always liked us to look good on the outside. She polished my saddle shoes daily, and I remember the special dresses she had my sister and me wear. She spent most of her waking hours trying to mask what was going on in our home.

I remember fearing what each day would bring. I remember the police coming to our door and my brother and sister and me having to hide in the bathroom with my dad.

I was a very sensitive child. I once spent all afternoon searching in the grass for a snake I had seen, to give him a drink of water. His tongue was constantly going in and out of his mouth, so I thought he was thirsty.

I also spent a long time – many years – searching for an identity and most of all for love, acceptance, and a place to belong.

During my childhood I was broken and angry inside. When I was seven years old and we were living in Edmonton, I came home from school and saw a moving truck parked in front of our house. I was given a choice of which parent I wanted to go with. I asked where my sister, Terry, was going. She and I went with Mom. My brother, David, also came with us, but later he chose to live with Dad.

The next two years, living with Mom and her new husband, Denny, were quite normal. We were up north in Fort Smith, Northwest Territories, a very small town of maybe two thousand people. I now had a new baby sister, Denise. The four of us lived in a hotel that Denny was managing. I felt some security and excelled at school. We then moved back to Edmonton, and I went to a new school. I thought everything was going to be okay.

One weekend when I was nine my mother sent David (he was now back living with us), Terry, and me to my grandparents' house for a visit. On Sunday night, when Grandpa dropped us off at our home, I ran up the walkway eager to see my mom. Outside our house was a landing with three stairs, at the top of which you could look into the kitchen. When I got there I could see there was nothing there. The house was bare. I ran from room to room searching. I started crying uncontrollably.

My grandfather followed me in and read a note that was sitting in the kitchen for my father: "It is your turn to look after the kids," it said. My mom had taken her new husband and my baby sister and left. I would not hear from her for another year.

So David, Terry, and I lived with our grandparents for the next year. These were my dad's parents. If they had not taken us in, we would have been placed with social services. Grandma and Grandpa were very good to us, and I felt safe with them. My father came to visit occasionally and said he was going to take us to live with him but first needed to build a house. He, too, had remarried.

I missed my mom and began to act out. I was

always fighting at school. No one took the time to find out why. I would go off for hours alone, walking. During one of those walks I found a rosary and decided that someday I would become a nun. One Sunday I decided to go to church. God was never a part of our daily lives. I didn't even know where I should go. I remembered that my mom had taken us to a church when I was maybe six. So I walked there – it was a long ways away – and sat down just inside the front doors. I found one of those Good News Bibles and started looking at it. Nobody paid any attention to me. I felt all alone, so I got up and walked home.

Mom phoned after almost a year. I was so excited to hear from her. I can still picture the telephone table and me anxiously waiting for my turn to talk to her. I don't remember the exact words we spoke, but I do remember how happy I was.

My father was true to his word. He moved us in with him and his new wife. She was now pregnant with my little brother, Chris. But things fell apart between my father and his wife. She left with her baby, leaving us with Dad.

During that time Mom's husband had been drinking and was killed in a head-on collision. Mom came back to Edmonton, and she and my dad thought being together again was the answer to all their problems. This period of my life, just as when I was younger and we were all together, was filled with anger and fear.

One night the two of them went out and Dad came home very early the next morning, alone, with a moving truck. I kept shouting, "Where's my mother?" as I watched the furniture leave again. I took a rolling pin and tried to beat my father, which of course earned me the honour of being kicked out with Mom.

During all this I could feel an impenetrable wall forming around me, one that would lead me to many poor choices and much emotional pain.

By this time I was twelve years old and began a stint of living in a townhouse in Edmonton with my mom, David, and Terry. Mom had a new boyfriend, Bill. We tried to act like a normal family, going out for dinner together, camping, going on outings. Inside, though, I was angry. Nobody could tell me anything. I had no respect for my mom and didn't trust her – or for that matter any adult. I began skipping school and staying out all night. By the time I turned thirteen, I had begun experimenting with drugs.

It was around this time that I read the book *Go Ask Alice*, a fictional diary of a teenage girl on drugs. This book only fuelled my desire to take drugs.

I ended up in a children's centre, the next step in my progression to serious drug-taking. Children of all ages lived at this centre. Some, like me, were runaways, with nowhere to go or were waiting to be placed in a foster home. I met someone there who glorified drugs. I got out and found the people she had told me about. I remember that night so clearly. The beat-up duplex, the people there passing a needle around. When it was my turn, I stuck out my arm, closed my eyes, and felt the most wonderful calmness flow into me. I quickly grew dependent on that feeling to make me feel safe inside.

These people who adopted me into their "family" gave me the name Sweet Baby Jane. I felt I finally had an identity and a place to belong. I thought these people truly cared about me.

At fifteen I took things up – or down – a notch and became a prostitute downtown. I didn't feel good about doing this, but it was the next logical step on my journey into a world I had decided was right for me. I stood on the corner with the other girls in the cold Edmonton winter. I kept trying to get off drugs, but I had become dependent on the person I was when I was high. I thought drugs were giving me freedom, but in reality they were trapping me.

In the midst of all this I decided to spend Christmas with my father. We fell into the role of being Daddy and daughter and everything seemed fine – until the alcohol came out. Not a good scenario. Suffice it to say that I found myself running through the snow back to the comfort and safety of my street family. Back to the place where no one would hurt me. Back to where I was loved and accepted.

Or so I thought. That proved to be an illusion when I was abused by one of my housemates. On the move again, I went to Victoria to live with a family friend, Donna. I arrived with two black eyes and a lot of emotional bruising. I got back into school, got a boyfriend, and tried not to do drugs. I did all the things a good teenage girl was supposed to be doing. After a year in Victoria, however, the pull to go back to Edmonton was too great to resist.

So I returned and got back into school, but I didn't feel I belonged there, either. It was not long before I gave my old friends a call. They were certainly more than welcoming. The drugs, the needle, and the spoon. So much easier than trying to fit in at school. It was just too hard pretending that I was living, and could live, a normal life.

I eventually ended up going out with a biker, a member of the Grim Reaper motorcycle club. We moved in together. To understand how messed up I was, consider this: I thought being with this man was a way to clean up my life. It was not long before I lured him into my way of living, instead. I had no control over my urge to use drugs. Soon he was seduced by my addictions. When I realized that I was going to destroy him, I left.

Where to go? Back to the streets and prostitution. I even tried working as a cocktail waitress. But I always found myself drawn back to the drugs. I would get high – and stay high for days.

The problem was, I was getting tired of struggling to make ends meet. I needed money. I was surrounded by men who glamourized stealing, and so I began robbing drug stores and even a bank. I loved the thrill of it, and the fact that people admired me for my courage. It gave me the sense of belonging I was always searching for. As for the consequences of my actions, I didn't think too much about that.

My career as a Bonnie was very short. Perhaps I needed a Clyde to work with. At the tender age of twenty-one I was given a jail sentence of thirteen years for my efforts. The year was 1981 and the judge decided what my next destination would be: the infamous Prison for Women, in Kingston, Ontario.

I now lived in a six by eight cell that contained only a bed, a steel blue dresser, a toilet, and a fluorescent light that never went out. There were only two showers for fifty women in our part of the jail. At first I put on a brave front, telling myself that my identity was not there in my cell in this prison – that it was in my heart waiting to be born. I would look in the mirror in my cell and boldly say to myself, "I am doing thirteen years," trying to defy the reality of my situation and take control of my surroundings. I promised myself I would not be defeated. The irony was that I already was defeated.

My first few months there were full of fear and uncertainty. In my first week, three girls jumped another girl and stabbed her. I grew accustomed to the usual prison events: stabbings, hangings, riots, women slashing other women, women crying to see their children. I also grew accustomed to my new life. I had to leave my cell during the day, but at night I stayed close to the range and my cell. It did not take me long to make friends. The other inmates and the guards were now my new family. I actually started feeling comfortable being locked up. Too comfortable.

It would be five years before I received my first parole. I was released to a Vancouver halfway house. I remember getting off the plane and saying to my parole officer, "You should get rid of the no-alcohol stipulation – otherwise I'm not going to make it on the outside."

At the halfway house I looked around and thought, "How do they expect me to clean up my act putting me here with other women from prison?"

Sure enough, I ended up going downtown, where of course I was a hero to the people on the street. How did they reward me for my bravery in going to prison? With the needle, the spoon, and the drugs. I was back on the merry-go-round, and society rewarded me by sending me back to prison.

This time I went to Oakalla Prison, in Burnaby, B.C. I waited six months there for the prisoners' flight to transport me back to Kingston. Out of this experience I decided I would not take another day parole. I was going back to do the rest of my time, another two years. That way I would not have to be supervised when I was released and would have more choice in where I would go. When that day finally came, my mom and her new husband, Cliff, welcomed me to their home in Victoria. I was never to return to prison again.

I did not realize how much of a toll prison had taken on me. I found it difficult to sleep in a non-prison bed – the mattress was too soft. Once when I went out for brunch at a fancy restaurant downtown with my mom, Cliff, and Denise, I had to get out and walk around the block until they finished. The ceilings were too low for me. I also found I could not talk properly into an answering machine. I had to learn to drive all over again.

But eventually I thought my life was going okay. I began to go Narcotics Anonymous meetings, where I met other people I could relate to. I began a serious relationship with one of the men in the group and we moved into an apartment together. I began learning a trade from Cliff, tile-setting, and I even bought myself a new truck. I was volunteering at the youth detention centre.

Then one night when I was in Vancouver for the weekend I found myself in a bar drinking. I had been clean and sober for years. But I got so drunk that night. I had left my relationship and was on to the next one. At this point I had no spiritual, emotional, or mental defences against anything. I had attracted a man who ended up beating me. I ended up lying in a ditch by the Pat Bay Highway outside Victoria, after one of those beatings.

I went to a transition house for battered women, but I still went back to him.

That relationship ended and I moved in with a woman who I thought was safe. She was not. She was using drugs, though to her credit she tried to hide the fact from me. The thought of using again had not entered my mind, but as soon as I realized it was right there so close to me, it was all I could think about. I welcomed the relief of being high. I only wanted to block out how I felt. Just one more time, just one more time – that was the lie I always told myself.

I really wanted to climb out of my addiction. I did not know how.

People along the way had tried to help me. I just did not believe anybody could love me. I had tried going to church, where people told me Jesus could help me. I thought they were all nuts. It was okay for them, but not for me.

One night all that changed. I was in a motel alone, desperately trying not to use. I was lying on my back staring up into the darkness. I actually cried out to God to help me. You can imagine my surprise when he answered me. How? I had a vision in which I was a very young girl dancing in a magnificent light at the bottom of a well. I did not know what it meant.

A few days later I received a letter in the mail from Cliff, Mom's husband. He knew nothing about my vision, or maybe he did, spiritually. He said he was prompted to write me the meaning. "Janie, if you look closely at the sides of the well," he wrote, "you will see all the people's faces who have prayed for you over the years, and when you get to the top of the well, you will see that the solid rock is Jesus Christ."

I knew then that God was real. He had revealed himself to me. It no longer was someone telling me about him. I met him myself. Now I had hope.

My life began to change. I have not put a needle in my arm since that night. The desire to use had been replaced. I am not saying my life is perfect. I am saying that now I have my heavenly Father to rely on. He does not beat me or lie to me. He wants only the best for me.

And he has given me a place to belong.

Carol Andrews

BECOMING FREE
INSIDE

I was born on June 20, 1965, in Hamilton, Ontario. I know very little about my biological mother. I was adopted by foster parents when I was ten days old and was the youngest of six kids in their family. Two others – two boys – were also adopted.

Our group of eight lived on a mink farm in the township of Pelham, about twenty minutes' drive from the city of St. Catharines, Ontario, in the Niagara Peninsula. We kept about five thousand mink on our five-acre spread. We were a good Mennonite family who faithfully attended the Fairview Mennonite Brethren Church nearby.

I became a Christian at around the age of twelve and was baptized at our church when I was about fourteen. One summer, when I was in my early teens, I did some youth ministry work with

Friendship Ministries, which involved singing and helping to operate some puppet shows.

We moved into St. Catharines when I was fourteen or so. The farm work was getting too hard for my dad, and he wanted to retire. My sister and her family took over the farm, though because money was tight my dad did have to continue working on it. At first I hated the city, but I got used to it.

I started high school at a Mennonite school called Eden Christian College, then located in Virgil, near Niagara-on-the-Lake. After one year I was forced by lack of money to switch to a public high school.

At around this time, things weren't going well with mink farming. My parents were getting further and further into debt. They were losing everything they had worked so hard for. Dad cried at night. He had to borrow money from my grandparents to put food on the table until things were settled with the bank. I was the only child still at home and still in school.

In the midst of all this I started frequenting downtown St. Catharines. I hung out at precisely the places I should have avoided: bars, the bus terminal, and the cab stands. In 1981, when I was sixteen, I started seeing a man who was in his mid to late forties. After a few months with him, I quit school and moved in with him. I thought he was my way out – that this arrangement would help my parents out financially.

My biggest mistake was not talking to them about how I was feeling. I felt I was a burden because of everything they were going through. I thought it would be better if I wasn't at home. A lot of what I was going through was probably par for the course for a teenage girl, but it was more than that in my case: I was rebelling against my parents and against their church. I didn't know it at the time, but I was already nicely down the road to prison.

By this time I hadn't been going to church for several years. I was living life my own way. I had started my lifetime habit of smoking cigarettes at age twelve. There was no question about going back to church and my former life. Living with a man unmarried was just not acceptable behaviour. Some members of the church came to our house and tried to talk to me, but I wouldn't listen.

My parents, in spite of everything they were going through, stayed close to God. I, on the other hand, did not. I couldn't understand how God could let such terrible things happen to people who were so faithful to him. In the end, my non-attendance and my relationship caused me to lose membership in my church. (To use Mennonite terminology, I was excommunicated.) At the time I didn't care. A lot of people who called themselves Christians acted no better than anyone else. I didn't want anything to do with church. I wasn't interested in what they were selling.

My relationship with this man was pretty normal, other than the fact that it was composed of a married man with a drinking problem and a rebellious teenager three decades his junior. In any case, it ended after three years. I remember the day it happened. It was my nineteenth birthday and I was out that evening with a friend, because my partner was at home, incapacitated by drinking. When I got home, he was passed out in bed. An empty case of beer and forty-ounce bottle of rye were lying nearby.

I came to shortly after falling asleep to find myself being pulled out of bed by my feet. He was awake and was spoiling for an argument. I obliged. Our "talk" must have gotten pretty loud because someone called the cops in. I wasn't surprised. It wasn't the first verbal battle between us.

The police took me to the hospital to be checked for injuries, which turned out to be a few scratches and bruises. They made me promise not to go back to the house that night. I wasn't supposed to call him, either, but when we got to the hospital the nurses told me he had been calling all night. So, with the police standing by, I got him on the line and told him I would not be returning that night or any night.

I called my parents and my mom came and picked me up at the hospital. No charges were laid. The next day I went to the house and got all my things and never went back.

I stayed with my parents, peacefully, but moved into my own apartment in the city a few months later. I got a job working in a pizza place close to where I lived. I also drove cab and worked in a bar. At this point I had to have three jobs on the go just to cover my basic needs and pay the bills.

Two years later I moved in with a General Motors worker. He worked in St. Catharines but had a house in Welland. I was twenty-one, and he was in his forties.

I'm not sure why my relationships were always with older men. The men involved were fairly stable and had jobs, so I didn't have to pay rent. That was part of it, I suppose. They were married, which meant marrying each other wasn't an option. That was fine with me, so that was probably part of it, too. I would end up spending nine years with this man.

After six years of working those three low-paying jobs, I got a better job, as an injection moulding press operator in a rubber plant in St. Catharines, making $12 an hour. I continued to drive cab part time, for extra money for Christmas. I worked at the rubber plant for six years, during which time I was able to purchase my own taxi plate and put my own taxi on the road. Shortly after that, the plant was closed, so the taxi became my only source of income.

My live-in and I were both working a lot. Four years into our relationship, things weren't going well between us, but we still had another five years together ahead of us.

A few years later, while we were still together, I started having an affair with a friend, a taxi broker. He was in his mid-fifties and married with one married son and several grandchildren. My partner and I finally parted ways. We divided our possessions, and I moved back to St. Catharines.

The affair continued but was soon to come to an end – a bad end. I was three months short of being thirty years old. I was taking prescription medications – Prozac and Atavan – that later were proven to be dangerous when taken together.

I will never forget the night of March 25, 1996.

My boyfriend was at my house after work. I had just purchased this house and there were renovations to be done. I had finished the apartment in the basement myself and had already rented it out. Now my boyfriend and I were working on a bedroom that I was going to rent out on the first of April to a friend I knew from driving taxi.

During the dinner I made for the two of us, my boyfriend lit into me about how the basement tenant had not been giving me his phone messages. He summed up his part of the argument by saying, "I want you to kick him out." I summed up mine by saying, "I can't just do that. There are laws about giving notice."

He became very upset and left the kitchen to prepare the spare room for painting. I started to put supper away and was moving some things around, including a .22 caliber rifle, which I was going to put in the attic. I had paid my $50 and acquired a FAC licence from the police station. The licence gave me the right to purchase a rifle without having any safety training in handling or storing it. My plan was to learn how to hunt.

Just then my boyfriend called me to the spare room to ask me where something was. I put the gun down to go talk to him, but when he said, "Never mind, I found it," I picked it up again. Then he came right back in to ask me something else. As I turned around to answer him, I don't know what happened, but the gun discharged and the bullet hit him in the neck.

I panicked but kept my senses enough to call 911 and then go to his side to try to stop the bleeding. The police and ambulance arrived within minutes, but it was too late. He was dead.

I was arrested and charged with manslaughter. The charge was then upgraded, first to second-degree murder and then to first-degree murder. I don't know why. Maybe because he was married and still living with his wife and they thought I had been trying to get him to leave her for me. That was not true, though. I didn't want another live-in relationship. I was quite happy with the way things were.

I spent three months in the Barton Street Detention Centre in Hamilton waiting for bail. During that time I did a lot of thinking and praying for God's help. My family somehow scraped enough funds together to hire a well-known lawyer to represent me. I was released on bail on June 12, 1996.

While I was waiting for my trial I got a part-time job doing volunteer maintenance work at a Mennonite old age home. I started going back to my old church. I lived with my parents for one month during this time, and then with my sister and her husband until my trial was over. I felt I was back on the right track, getting back to my Mennonite roots and living the lifestyle required of me.

Being good Christians, my parents never gave up on me. My mom kept praying for me. She told me that at one point she had said to God while she was going to the grocery store once, "Lord, I have done all I can; I now put her into your hands."

The Lord showed me that my judgment of the church people was wrong. The very people that I thought were hypocrites were standing behind me and supporting me and my parents. They accepted me back into the church and tried to help me any way they could, all the way through my trial and incarceration. The Lord gave me good friends just when I needed them most.

My trial began in February 1997. The police and the prosecutors did not believe that the shooting was accidental and that I had not meant to hurt anyone. The night before the trial, I asked God to set me free, but he had other plans.

The trial lasted for two weeks. On March 3, 1997, I was convicted of second-degree murder. In April 1997 I was sentenced to life in prison, with a minimum of ten years in custody before the possibility of full parole. The jury had recommended a minimum of fifteen years, but the judge, taking into consideration all the letters the court had received from my family and friends, reduced it.

God always answers prayers, but sometimes the answer is not what we want to hear. He answers yes or no, or, as in my case, "You've got to be kidding."

What was going to happen to me now? I was taken into custody immediately and reintroduced to the Barton Street Detention Centre. I was transferred from there to the Toronto West Detention Centre, where I spent the worst three weeks of my life. And things weren't going to get better anytime soon: The next stop on my itinerary was the notorious Prison for Women in Kingston, Ontario.

When I arrived at P4W and those big steel doors slammed behind me, I knew I needed God now more than ever. P4W was a very old, rundown building.

My new home was a six by nine cell with bars and an old army cot for a bed. My bathroom was right there in the cell. The prison was on its last legs. There were only about ten inmates there. It didn't take long for me to get to know some of them.

I was introduced to the Mennonite minister who visited the prison, a very nice man. I got to know a woman in the chaplaincy program and found I could talk to her. She was also in charge of the Christian-based programs at the prison.

P4W closed three months after I arrived there. I had been assessed as not being a security risk, so I was transferred to Grand Valley Institution for Women in Kitchener, Ontario. This was on August 27, 1997.

In 2000 I filed an appeal against my conviction and sentence. I asked God to set me free. His response, along with the government's, was, "Not yet." I had seven years to go.

It was at Grand Valley that I really started to grow. God was setting me free on the inside. I was doing a number of Bible studies to learn as much as I could to forgive myself for what happened. I attended chapel regularly and prayed for others.

Another appeal was heard four years later, in 2004, and dismissed. I proceeded with an appeal to the Supreme Court of Appeals, but by then I was about to come up for my day parole, so I dropped it. (Day parole is part of a series of more and more time away from jail or a halfway house with less and less supervision, on the way to full parole.)

During my time in prison, I witnessed a lot of tough situations. I saw women high on drugs and drunk on homemade brew. I saw women slash their wrists and get beat up so badly they almost died. I saw a woman hang herself. The list goes on and on, and at any time I could have been on it. The prison system doesn't do anything to minimize the danger to inmates. They know what's going on – there are plenty of people who report trouble to the staff – but they don't do much to prevent it. When they do take action, it's usually too late.

People like to think that life is easy in the new prisons, but they're wrong. My time in prison was never easy. I needed God's help and protection just to survive my sentence. I thank God I wasn't one of those women who were beaten so badly they feared for their lives. I was lucky.

I have had a hearing impairment since I was twenty-one, bequeathed to me by my biological mother. I underwent three surgeries to correct it before going to prison. The last one was not long before my arrest and I had not yet been fitted for hearing aids. When I entered the prison system I couldn't hear much at all, which put me at even greater risk. I had my hearing tested and was prescribed hearing aids. I needed them in order to participate in programs and do my schooling and work, but the correctional system said it would not pay for them. They were going to cost about $5,000, and Corrections said my family would have to pay for them, which just wasn't possible. I was making $6.90 a day, so it wasn't as if I was going to be able to buy them.

Through the complaint system and with the help of advocacy groups I began to fight the correctional system to accommodate my disability. It took about two years, but I won, praise God. In the process I caused Corrections to change their national guidelines to provide hearing aids for inmates across Canada. It was a very long road to getting this policy changed, and being the trailblazer wasn't easy. But my persistence paid off. With God's help anything is possible.

While I was incarcerated I followed a "correctional plan" involving programs and school work. Participation was required in order to get paid, which was the only way of getting money for cigarettes, personal items, your share of the cable TV, and so on. Ten percent of my pay was put in a savings account.

A desire grew in me to acquire knowledge and begin living the life I should have been living before I was arrested. Besides participating in Bible studies, I took courses in anger management and cognitive living skills and attended the Alternatives to Violence program. I also received psychological counselling, as well as counselling with the Canadian Hearing Society. I graduated with a grade twelve diploma. I played bass guitar in chapel services. I took peer support training to help other inmates in crisis situations. I took mediation training, an employment course, and a course with Tri-County Truck Driver Training. I received my snowplow operator's licence and my commercial custodial diploma.

In fact, between my incarceration in 1997 and my release on day parole in 2004, I received sixty-three certificates and diplomas.

I rededicated my life to God in 1998. I know I never would have made it in prison without him in my life. God has forgiven me, but the hard part is forgiving myself for being so careless in handling the gun that took a life.

I thank God for each and every loving and

supportive person he has put in my life, and for all the prayers and support that have been granted me and my family. The Lord has brought me through many difficult times, and has changed my life. He has opened many doors for me over the years. He took me from maximum security to minimum security in just one year. That was so unusual it could only have been the direct result of his will.

God has always been in control, and always will be in control. He is my strength and hope, and I thank him for the wisdom and courage he has given me to change my life. I know he will provide the strength I need to return to society.

And I will always know that God and mothers have a special bond – that he listens to a mother's prayer for her children. So children, beware of your mother's prayer, because he will use it to get your attention.

I was released on day parole on the afternoon of Friday, September 3, 2004. I arrived at the halfway house in Dundas, Ontario, where I've been staying ever since.

At the time of my release, my father was very sick and in the hospital. He had diabetes and was having his feet amputated, plus he had had a few heart attacks. I saw my parole officer the same afternoon and requested a day pass to visit him in the hospital the next day. The pass never came. At 8 a.m. on that Sunday, I received a phone call from my mom. She told me that Dad had died.

Dad had held on long enough to know I was released. Once he knew I was safe, he was ready to go. I wasn't ready for him to go, though. I wish I'd had the chance at least to say goodbye.

For the week of the funeral, I was granted leave from the halfway house to be with my family, and my curfew was extended from 6 p.m. to 11 p.m. I was so proud to be a pallbearer for my dad. He was my biggest supporter throughout my life, and whatever I did, he was always so proud of me. I will never forget the day in 2000 when I finally graduated from grade 12. He came to the graduation. He was so proud of me – he bragged and bragged about me. I miss my father greatly. I know he would be so proud of me today for all I've accomplished.

After the funeral I began looking for a job. The Lord opened a door for me again, and in October 2004 I started working in a factory making balloons. I am still working there today. I bought a car so I could commute from Dundas to Stoney Creek for work and visit my family in St. Catharines.

I have started speaking in high schools, universities, and colleges. I talk about the prison system and the misconceptions society has about how the new prisons are set up, as well as about my life. By the time this book is out, I should be on full parole. After that I will see what the next chapter of my life holds for me. My plans are to go home and spend as much time as I can with my elderly mother. I couldn't be with my dad in his time of trouble, but maybe I can make up for that by being with my mom. I am active in my home church again. I'm holding my own. It has been a struggle, but with God's help, I know I will prevail.

~ Becoming Free Inside ~

Stacey-Ann Bucknor

My Lost
Decade

*Would it surprise you
if I told you I value
stability more than
anything else in the
world? After what I've
gone through, doing the
same thing every day
with the same people
around me – the ones
I love – well, to me
that's not just a taste of
heaven, that is heaven.*

---

*~ This story is by the daughter of Vivienne Nash,
whose story also appears in this book.* ~ Editor

I have lived all of my twenty-four years either in or on the border of Toronto's Jane-Finch neighbourhood. Yes, in one of the city's most dangerous areas. I sometimes wonder how many times Torontonians have heard the words on television: "Another gang-related killing in the Jane-Finch Corridor. Details at 11."

However, most of us who live in this neighbourhood see our lives as normal. We are busy trying to keep up financially in a part of the city given over to low-paying jobs in the manufacturing, service, and retail sectors. Kids still go to school every day. Parents still go to work – or spend time looking for work. In fact, even if your own life is touched by "Jane-Finch crime," very few of the people around you know about it. As far as they are concerned, you're just like everyone else: trying to better your life and otherwise doing what you can to get through each day.

There. I just described myself in those last two sentences. Beginning very early in my life, I was touched by crime. My mom was a drug runner and spent some long stretches in jail. I was never taunted at school for having a mother who was in trouble with the law. No one really knew.

And I wasn't pitied for having to travel from home to home as I grew up. During various parts of those early years I lived with my father and his mother, my mother and her mother, just with my mother, just with my grandmother, and even, for a time, with a family friend near Jane and Eglinton to the south of all these other places.

You could say it's part of my culture for kids to grow up with friends and relatives instead of with their own parents. But when you're a kid growing up, you don't care about culture. You don't even know what it is. You just want to be with your parents – or at least with one of them.

All of this happened during my lost decade, the period from when I was four to when I was fourteen – a time that coincided with my mother's own lost decade. Hers began with drug running and incarceration in a jail in Jamaica; continued with some skirmishes with the law in Canada, resulting in another jail sentence; and ended in a spiritual breakthrough. That breakthrough has freed her from the cycle of crime and punishment – and has made my life what I always wanted it to be.

∞

I remember very little from my preschool years, except for one major event. I was four and was deeply in love with Barbie dolls. One day, to my great surprise, my mother actually gave me one. I was so happy to get that doll. Mom just threw her head back and laughed as I practically pummelled her with hugs and thank-yous.

"I'm so pleased you like your new doll, sweetie," she said, when she caught her breath. And then she started laughing again.

A few minutes later she told me, "Stacey, baby, Mommy's going on a trip now, but she's going to come right back to see her little girl, the sweetest little girl in the whole wide world."

But she didn't come right back, and I couldn't figure out why. I knew my mom loved me – the Barbie doll, to my small mind, being the latest proof of the fact. I knew that she kept her promises to me. So why didn't she come back right away? Was it maybe that I *wasn't* the sweetest girl in the whole wide world?

Gradually I put it together that Mom was in jail in Jamaica for something bad she had done. I got to talk to her on the phone a few times during the sixteen months of her imprisonment. Each time we spoke I was so excited. During our conversation the sun rose way, way up in the bluest of skies. When she hung up, another long period of turbulence came rolling in. I was so afraid. I was so sad.

My father and mom had never gotten married, but during this time he was granted custody of me. For several years I spent weekdays with him in the apartment he shared with his mother and spent weekends with my grandmother at her apartment. I wasn't happy at my father's. If I had known what TGIF meant, I would have said it every Friday morning the moment I opened my eyes. All week I longed for Friday evening when Grandma, my mother's mother, after finishing her day at the factory where she worked and taking the bus to my dad's, took me to her place.

The only constant in my life was my grand-mother. In fact, she wanted to keep me with her during this time but couldn't afford to. My dad said it was better if he took care of me – he said he didn't have the extra money to give Grandma to hire a babysitter for when she was at work.

I loved being with Grandma. She took *wonderful*

care of me. At times she may have even spoiled me, but that's what grandmas are for, right? I remember the mornings we spent together on the weekends. She would make a big breakfast for us and then we'd watch cartoons on TV and just laugh and laugh. But then Sunday evening would come around again, and it was back to dad's I would go.

I was so excited when Grandma told me Mom was coming home. Just after she landed back in the city, she came over on the bus to pick me up. I screamed and went running to her. I jumped into her arms for the longest, sweetest hug a Mommy and daughter had ever experienced. Then she and I took the bus to Grandma's apartment, where the three of us soaked up every minute of the weekend together. I don't think we left the premises once the whole time.

Shortly after this, Mom succeeded in getting custody of me, so when I was six, with the two of us living together with Grandma, things started looking up. But a strong undercurrent was always trying to claim me. As I went through my primary school years and then entered junior high, I had a pretty good idea Mom was doing things that might get her into trouble again. I was angry when she went out late at night – sometimes she'd be gone for days on end. "What's wrong with me?" I wanted to ask her. "Why can't you just be happy being with me? Do you love your friends more than you love me?"

When she did get into trouble again – this time in Canada, when I was twelve years old – I was much more aware of her predicament, and mine. This time there was no Barbie doll and there was no fond embrace. I was at a family friend's apartment on Eglinton Avenue to the south of our place waiting for Mom to pick me up. But she didn't show up. I could tell something was wrong. Phone calls kept coming in and my friend looked worried. Grandma came to get me and took me to her apartment. Then my father came to get me and take me to his apartment. There was a big commotion as he and Grandma talked while he pulled my stuff together.

This time Mom was away for eighteen months. I never got to go see her – I couldn't afford the trip. I was always so happy when I was able to talk to her on the phone. But as before, stormy weather took over as soon as the call was over.

Shortly after Mom got out of prison this time, I began to see something in her life – a happiness, a contentedness, a determination to stay on the straight and narrow – that I hadn't seen before. I was cautiously optimistic, as the diplomats are fond of saying about peace in the Middle East. I hoped that this change was for real, but guarded myself from disappointment just in case it wasn't.

A couple of years before this, Grandma and I had begun attending Faith United Church of God every Sunday morning. My godmother was a member there and introduced us to this small church of under 100 people. I remember not wanting to go. The worship service seemed so long. But hearing the good news that was preached from the pulpit and feeling the love of the people began to speak to my heart. I responded to an altar call at the end of a service and gave my heart to the Lord. Everyone came up to the altar and prayed with me, telling me how much God loved me and how much they loved me.

Mom came to church with us from time to time and then started attending another church regularly. I became more and more optimistic, and less and less cautious, about the changes I could see in her life and what they could mean for our future together.

When she committed her life to the Lord and began her ministry to prisoners and ex-prisoners, speaking in public to raise support for them, I threw both optimism and cautiousness to the winds and replaced them with faith and belief. I knew that God had transformed me, and I knew that he had transformed my mother, and I knew that he was transforming our relationship, too.

My mom really has turned her life around. We are all very proud of her. We're not afraid that she'll go back to her old life. God is in her life now. She will not go down that road again.

Would it surprise you if I told you I value stability more than anything else in the world? After what I've gone through, doing the same thing every day with the same people around me – the ones I love – well, to me that's not just a taste of heaven, that *is* heaven.

Because of Grandma's influence, I was a diligent student and steered a wide berth around kids who could have gotten me into trouble. I finished high school at age seventeen and took half a year off school, working at a big theater complex to the north of our apartment while figuring out what my next step would be.

I ended up studying nursing for three years at George Brown College in downtown Toronto, and now work as a registered nurse at St. Michael's Hospital, also downtown. I work in six-week cycles: four weeks of days, from 7:30 in the morning to 7:30 at night, and then, after a weekend off, two weeks of nights, working from 7:30 at night till 7:30 in the morning. My dream is to work in an Intensive Care Unit, which will require a year of further coursework.

Mom and I live together in the apartment I have lived in now since the age of thirteen. Grandma is only twenty minutes away and we talk on the phone every day and get together every chance we can. I'm on good terms with my dad – in fact, recently he and I looked back on those dramatic times when Mom first went to jail. Both of us have a better perspective on that time now.

So now I have everything I need in life: faith in God; a wonderful church family; a mother able to devote herself to me – as a friend now, really; my adorable grandma nearby; and a career that I enjoy very much.

It takes me an hour to get to my job in the hospital by bus and subway. Once I'm in transit, I plug in my earphones, turn on my trusty Walkman, and

Christina

GIRL

INTERRUPTED

*Most people do not
understand the impact
of a family breakdown
like ours. Unless they
have experienced
something like it
themselves, there's no
way they can grasp
the demented merry-
go-round ride called the
criminal-justice system
that it puts you on.*

---

*~ This story is by the daughter of Dewey, whose
story also appears in this book. ~* Editor

L IKE everyone else, I have a bad day every once in a while.

I love my job but sometimes a particularly hectic day at work can get to me. I am a manager of customer service at one of the five major financial institutions in downtown Toronto. Or sometimes I'm a bit down because it's 6 a.m. and I'm getting into a cold car to drive to the subway station for the commute to work. As the car and I struggle to get some warmth into our bones, I groan at the thought that I won't be back in my nice warm house for another thirteen or fourteen hours.

Where I may be different from most people, however, is that I know, no matter how bad things get, that I will survive. I've been through far worse – *far* worse – and survived. In fact, I went through a wrenching experience as a young woman, an incident that led to the death of my father, the imprisonment of my mother, and an all-out battle on my part to retain custody of my two brothers, who are ten and thirteen years younger than me.

I was nineteen when this happened, just a couple of months into my first year at the University of Toronto. I had attended Roman Catholic schools right through high school. I was a serious student, on the honour roll most of the time. I graduated from high school as an Ontario Scholar. Before university, English was my favourite subject. Now I was planning to earn a double major, in sociology and the humanities.

At around Halloween, appropriately enough, I suppose, things started falling apart at home. I was angry at my father because he was having an affair. Call it a woman's intuition, but I knew about the affair before it came out into the open – perhaps even before my mother knew. I could tell from the way he was acting.

Exams were about to begin at school and I was actually looking forward to them. But I had to pull out because I knew I was needed at home.

One night during this time, I didn't know where

Mom was. I asked my father if he knew, and he said no. That's when I came right out and told him I was aware of what he was up to.

"If anything happens to her it will be your fault," I said. "You are my father by title, but that's where it ends. You have to earn it. You're no longer a part of me."

From then on, though we lived under the same roof, he avoided me. If I came into a room, he left shortly thereafter.

I was upset with my mom, too.

"You shouldn't just keep acting as if there is nothing wrong, protecting everyone from hurt feelings and protecting dad's secret," I said. "We have to get away from this. It's not just you he's betrayed. He has betrayed all of us."

Even though I was right in the middle of it, the situation didn't make sense to me. As a family we had been through some rough patches. Finances were always tight, mainly because my father often was not working. My younger brother's autism and special needs put a strain on the family, too.

Being that much older than my brothers, I was frequently able to take some pressure off my parents. I would babysit when my parents went on their frequent trips together or out for dinner on the weekends. They were thought of as a model married couple. They were a success story. People admired them for how they had kept the flame of romance burning long after their wedding day, in spite of getting married so young and having me so early in their marriage.

Then, just before Christmas, my mother told me that my father had admitted he was having an affair. She said that for her sanity's sake she had to get away for a while. She and my father were heading for a breakup, she said. She was going to have to leave my brothers with me and my father. Once she got her head together, and knew what her options were – especially with regard to programs she could access for my autistic brother – she would be back to get us.

During this time I sometimes heard my parents arguing – not that common an occurrence before this. They were so angry with each other. I sat on the stairs listening in case I had to go in to break things up.

Their arguments took the form of dad blaming mom for my knowing about his affair; his trying to exert control of her by telling her she could not leave; his warning her that his mother was never to find out about the affair; and then – and this one always threw me for a loop – his attempting to convince her that life could go on as normal, even though he had a girlfriend.

I knew the situation was serious but harboured hopes that their marital troubles were not terminal. I thought maybe I could keep things calm while Mom was away – she was planning to be with her sister in the U.S. for a while – and that when she returned she would somehow be able to patch things up.

∞

I just didn't understand – or didn't want to understand – how serious it was. Maybe they didn't, either.

Just before the Christmas holidays, they had a fierce row over her plans to leave. They were in their bedroom on the second floor. I was in my bedroom in the basement. They had renovated the basement for me when I went to university so I would have my own little place for studying and privacy.

I must have been asleep during the opening rounds. But when my mother let out a deathly yell, it pulled me right out of bed and before I knew it

I was running up the two flights of stairs to their room, calling "Mom" over and over again.

It was dark. I could hear them arguing, fighting, crying. By the time I entered their room, it had become physical. The two of them were covered with blood from knife wounds.

I separated them. I knew my mom was injured horribly because her face was bleeding and she had a huge black eye. I couldn't stop them from starting up again. Finally, they calmed down of their own accord and I found the weapon and took it downstairs.

Once there, I started to call the police. This was a very hard and confusing thing for me to do – I was calling the cops on my parents! But I was interrupted by the sounds of the fight breaking out again and hung up before anyone came on the line. I ran upstairs and pulled them apart.

Things got quiet then. Both were wounded and probably in shock. I was hugging my mother from behind. I knew life was never going to be the same.

"What am I supposed to do about this, Mom?" I cried. "What am I supposed to do about the kids?"

"Take care of them," she said. "Take care of them. Don't let them be separated."

Grandma must have called the police because I heard people coming up the stairs. I held my mom and kissed her, telling her that I loved her. The police came in the room, followed by the paramedics. I went to the next room – the kids' bedroom – and sat outside their door to keep it closed. I thought I had heard them getting up and I didn't want them to see what I had to see.

The police told me I should leave the area but I said I couldn't – I had to stay with the boys. They told me to stay in the room with them.

From their room, I heard my mom calling out to my dad. "Are you okay? I love you." Then, to my grandma, she said, "Are you okay? I'm sorry. I love you."

I spent the whole day at the police station, telling them they couldn't take the boys away from me – that I was of age to be their guardian. I knew I couldn't control what happened to my parents – in fact, by now I knew my dad was dead. But I felt that I could and had to control what happened to my brothers.

"You have no right to take them away," I kept saying over and over. I said the same thing to the Children's Aid workers when they were called in.

"You're right," one of them said when she could

get a word in. "We're not going to. You are well within your capability to take care of them."

These workers were actually quite good but I didn't trust anyone at this point. Over the next several days, I was on full alert for the slightest hint that the boys would be taken away from me.

Somewhere in the middle of all this, I met with our parish priest to help prepare my father's funeral service.

Meanwhile, I was trying to get the detectives who were assigned to the case to stop going through the motions and think it through. Their theory of what happened was just a little too easy, as far as I was concerned. My father was dead, so they didn't have to weigh both sides. It seemed to me they just wanted a story of convenience and not the truth.

"My mother is a peaceful, humble woman, who loves her family dearly," I said.

I kept asking them to take me to see her to make sure she was okay and to tell her we were okay, but they told me I was not allowed. I asked them to tell her that I loved her.

I was spending a lot of time with my brothers, trying to keep them calm, trying to help them understand why their daddy was dead and why they couldn't see their mommy. My explanations didn't help them much, but my presence did.

Sometimes I would just wrap them up in a blanket and sit with them watching cartoons.

A few days after the incident I buried my father, came back from Mass to change my clothes, and then went off to see my mother – finally, for the first time since she was taken into custody. Somehow, through the haze of the medication they were giving her to control her pain, she got it across to me that everything would be all right and that I had to keep the family together by being strong. She didn't realize that I was already a long way down that road.

Most young women have at least a few years between being a student and being a mother and full-time worker balancing their home and work responsibilities. I made that transition in an instant, during my mother's awful scream.

Finances were tough. I had to continue my full-time job to pay the bills and put food on the table. I tried going back to school once my mother was out on bail, but my family needed me too much and I had to quit again, losing another year of my education.

Even with the money that came in from my job, and the money we had saved, we didn't have the resources to procure the extra forensic investigations that would help get my mother acquitted.

While she was on bail a wonderful and very well-regarded lawyer tried to help her, even lowering his usual fees. He was sure of her innocence and felt for the family and the troubles we were going through. In fact, he actually cried with me in the corner of the courtroom when she had to enter a plea, leading to her prison term.

In the ensuing years, the only way I could protect my own sanity was to put these dramatic events into a file and put the file into a cabinet in a corner of my brain. While Mom was in prison I felt so alone. Sometimes the events would prey on me and convince me to get the file out and leaf through it. Once she was released from prison, I rarely looked at it. And now I've pretty much consigned it to the archives.

Things are much better now. My job is going well and I am finishing up my university degree part time. I am engaged and will be married soon. My fiancé and I plan to have a family, if God blesses us that way. And why not have a family? I've already been a mother, essentially. I will definitely know what to do.

Most people do not understand the impact of a

family breakdown like ours. Unless they have experienced something like it themselves, there's no way they can grasp the demented merry-go-round ride called the criminal-justice system that it puts you on.

In my case, my faith and my mother's love, strength, guidance, and training helped me survive that ride.

The night before my mom started her prison term, I spent a whole night in prayer at the altar in our parish church. I was in a sorry state. I had never felt so alone in my life.

I remember asking God during that long vigil, "Will we ever be together again as a family? Will we ever be happy together again?"

I'm very pleased to tell you that God heard my prayer that night.

The answer was yes.

Stephanie Martin

A Love
Better Than Drugs

MY name is Stephanie, and I am a recovering alcoholic, a recovering drug addict, an ex-con, and – oh yeah – now a born-again Christian. (I saved that one for last so as not to scare you away.)

These words are being typed in the classroom of a building located at the Grand Valley Institute for Women, better known as the Ontario women's prison. At this moment it has been 607 days since I have seen my daughter or any other member of my family (which in some cases is actually a good thing). It has also been 338 days since I last used any mind-altering substance, which for me is absolutely great news, but hard work, especially in my current living situation. And it is 394 days before I get to re-enter society.

I grew up in Pembroke, Ontario, and had a truly confusing childhood. How confusing? Well, I didn't know where I really lived, who my parents really were, or, at times, even what my name really was. I was born to a sixteen-year-old mother, Ann. She named me Stephanie Ann Marie. When a beautiful bouquet of flowers was delivered to our room at the hospital for my mother, the card was addressed to Ann and Stacey. Stacey? Apparently my great-grandmother really liked that name, got mixed up, and put it on the card. My family decided that instead of making Grandma feel foolish, they would just call me Stacey.

I lived at my grandma and grandpa's house with Mom, because, of course, she was too young to be out on her own with a young baby. But then, when I was only two years old, Mom moved out into her own apartment with her boyfriend. Although she was still in the same little town, she left me behind. I did, however, spend most of the time going back and forth between her apartment and my grand-parents' house. I suppose Mom's excuse was that she was too young to care for me properly. To my young mind, it didn't make any sense why she had abandoned me. All this took place before my mother decided to get married to the abovementioned boyfriend.

The latter happened when I was four. The groom seemed to be a nice enough chap, but he was not my father, though at this point I thought he was. I got to be the flower girl and wear a beautiful white dress, which looked adorable next to my blonde curls. I carried a bouquet of red roses. Next to the bride I was the most beautiful girl at the ball. But I was miserable the whole day. Perhaps I had a sixth sense about how bad things were going to be living with Mom and her amour, which I understood to be my fate.

Not long after the wedding, when I was five, my mother had another baby, and I learned that four's a crowd. Things weren't too bad for a while with me and my new sister in the household, but three years later we I got another sibling, a baby brother. Now we were a big happy family, right? Maybe not.

When I was around seven, my mother decided to get honest with me and tell me that her husband was not my father, and that my real father was a man I had never met. So, one day soon after that, it was off to McDonald's, of all places, to meet the mystery man, my natural father. As it turned out, I didn't like him at all – he wouldn't even buy me an ice cream sundae. After that awful first meeting, I didn't see my father again until I was about eleven, and since then he has come in and out of my life sporadically, whenever he feels the desire to be a dad for a few minutes.

But maybe the worst part of this revelation about my father was that it prompted the end of the honeymoon between me and my mother's husband. (Let's just call him "husband" from here on.) Now that husband knew I knew he wasn't my dad, he felt no further obligation to me. I suppose I probably acted like a brat sometimes, making the odd "I don't have to listen to you, you're not my father" comment. Not nice, I know, but I was a seven-year-old child, seriously confused by this point. Our relationship became even more antagonistic. Not knowing what else to do, Mom agreed that I should go back to Grandma and Grandpa's house.

I was with them for a few years but spent a lot of time bouncing back and forth between the two homes. Mom would get on these spurts when she'd think, "Things will be different this time." She would take me home with her and realize pretty quickly that, in fact, nothing had changed. So it was back to my grandparents' house I would go. I may as well have been a parcel from FedEx. At one point Mom even took me all the way out to Fort McMurray, Alberta. She had decided that Alberta was a good place to go, because two of her brothers, as well as husband, had relocated out there to find work, which they had been successful in achieving. This gave her the idea that we would all join them as one big happy family, a chance for a new beginning.

It was nice for a very short while, and then husband started to be unfaithful to my mother and things went from bad to worse very quickly. I lasted a sum total of one month in the wild west. I was returned to my grandparents after my behaviour became more than my mother could or would tolerate.

Mom stopped shipping me around when she finally divorced husband. After that she felt there was no longer any reason for me not to live with her, so I stayed with her consistently. This was not something I had any say in, and neither did my grandparents. By this time I was eleven, my sister was six, and my brother was three. We moved into a newly built complex for low-income families known as the Projects.

I found lots to do in the Projects. I started to hang out with the rest of the kids from the neighbour-hood, goofing off most of the time. I started to steal money from my mom's purse to buy cigarettes, to look cool to the other kids. As minuscule as I thought stealing a few bucks from her was, it turned out to be just the beginning of the nightmare that became my life.

For those few years I became the live-in baby-sitter for my sister and brother. This was not good for them. Remember, I had been ripped from my grandparents' home. I resented my mother, as well as my grandparents, for disrupting what I had come to know as my life. I expressed this anger mainly toward my younger siblings, because they were too small and vulnerable to fight back. I yelled at them, hit them, and was just plain cruel to them any time I had the chance.

Before long, at the ripe old age of twelve, I received my first criminal charge, for "theft of tele-communications." No, not for stealing a phone but for reversing the charges for long distance phone calls to another phone number, the number of a kid at school who picked on me all the time.

I had also found a phone number for a chat line, and when I started calling to chat, I was hooked by the ability to be anyone I wanted. These people didn't know me and believed anything I told them. I was very lonely at the time and the people on the other end of the phone became the friends I thought I was looking for.

These phone calls were extremely expensive, and when I figured out how to reverse the charges, I rang up my mother's phone bill, as well as my grandparents', to amounts well into the thousands of dollars. A lot of people were pretty upset with me for that little stunt, and the courts felt about the same way as the victims did. I was placed on probation for two years and given 200 hours of community service.

I figured that no decent kids would want to hang out with a troublemaker, which I now officially was because I had a criminal record. So I hung out with the bad kids and got into all kinds of trouble all the time. I realize now that I was just a lost little girl looking for some attention from the people who were supposed to love her. At the time, though, I thought I was simply unlovable. Even though the only thing I wanted in the world was my mother's love, I continued to rebel against everything she laid out for me. She got fed up. She could have sent me to Grandma's, like I wanted, but chose a group home, instead. She felt I was spoiled rotten living with her parents and she knew moving back there was what I wanted. She had sworn I would never live there again, and she planned to prove that she meant what she said.

So at thirteen I was in a group home with

Children's Aid Society children, kids doing open custody sentences, and kids who, like me, weren't wanted at home. If you ask my mother, she will tell you she was doing what she felt was best for me. She was probably being quite sincere about that, but unfortunately she didn't really know me at all.

I spent almost six months in this group home. Three days before I was scheduled to go home, I ran away with another one of the residents. When I was on the run, I was introduced to the world of drugs, and it was instant love. I had found that warm fuzzy feeling that I had been looking for. I had also found a group of people who accepted me for who I was (or so I thought, anyway).

I also experienced that feeling of love and acceptance when I returned, of my own accord, to my mother's home. When I walked through her door I finally felt love from her: it was the first time I can remember feeling it. She was crying and glad to see me, and it was the greatest thing I had ever experienced – better than drugs. I thought everything would be okay from then on, that we would be a happy family and she would never ever send me away again.

Then, reality.

After just an hour at home, my mother sent me back to the group home to finish off the time I had left in my "sentence": the whole three days. The group home had recommended that I return to finish my time, and she agreed. They had fed her some line about not giving in to my manipulative behaviour or I would use it all the time on her.

When I returned to my mother's three days later, it was as if the previous week's tearful reunion had never happened. Everything went right back to how it had been six months earlier. Once again I became the live-in babysitter for my siblings, and once again I started to feel like the mistake child. So about three months later, I ran away with my boyfriend.

This time I was gone for a month and made it to the big city of Ottawa, about 170 kilometers from Pembroke. I was scared out of my mind. For thirty days I fought to survive. The only thing that kept me going was the thought that the longer I was gone, the longer the feeling of euphoria and motherly love would last when I did go home again. Boy did I get that wrong. The warm fuzzy feeling from Mom must have been an aberration because, with one exception, I never felt it from her again.

The story of my early teens continues in a similar vein: I continued to rebel, run away, and get in trouble with the law, though now I started to drink more. Marijuana and hashish became a regular part of my lifestyle.

I spent many years in and out of open and secure young offenders' facilities, learning nothing in them except how to commit other crimes and which new drugs I should try when I got out. My life was a never-ending cycle of destruction. I mowed anyone down who crossed my path. I had begun to exist in a dark, dank world of self-loathing, self-destruction, and self-pity.

I hated everything about myself, and I did everything I could to push everyone who cared about me away. I felt I didn't deserve anything more than death. I would pray to a god I didn't believe existed to put me out of my misery and not let me wake up the next morning. But for the sake of torturing me, he let me wake up and continue to drown myself in the sludge and slime my life had become.

As the years went on, things got progressively worse. In 1997, when I was eighteen, I thought a change of geography might be the cure and moved to Windsor, Ontario. I had met a truck driver while hitchhiking with a friend down highway 401. He actually wanted to take care of me. He was a nice guy who worked for a small company out of Windsor. He was twenty-five and thought I was the sweetest girl in the world. I thought this was the best I could hope for, so off I went to live with him.

This was a cozy set-up for about three months, but pretty soon my lies and games caught up to me and caused the end of our relationship. I stayed in Windsor and found a roommate for a while, and then met a nice guy named Ted, a thirty-four-year-old mould maker, and moved in with him.

One day, about two months after Ted and I had been together, I started feeling sick. I thought, naive and melodramatic eighteen-year-old that I was, that I was deathly ill. As it turned out it wasn't anything death-related: it was something life-related. Yes, that's right: Miss Dysfunctional, the mayor of Dysfunctional City, the owner and operator of Dysfunctional International, was going to be a mother. "Lord, help this child," was all I could think. Of course, it was just my luck that I am against abortion, so I had only one option ... and baby makes three.

Or, in my case, makes two. At some point, I figure about a month after I found out I was pregnant, Ted left me. Once again my pattern of conning had caught up to me. Ted came home one day from work to find his apartment empty and his girlfriend in jail. The seller of our furniture, which I had purchased with a bounced cheque, had taken back what was rightfully his. This was very difficult for Ted to handle and I guess he figured that with everything else he had to deal with, he didn't need me in the mix. So, even though I was pregnant, he left.

I, meanwhile, was sentenced to sixty days in jail, my first adult conviction. I was alone and about to have a baby, and I was scared out of my wits. When I was released, I did what any single teenage girl all alone in a strange town and about to have a baby would do: run home as fast as her little legs would carry her.

So there I was, pregnant and back in Pembroke living with my mother. She was actually wonderful, standing with me through the entire ordeal, including the delivery of my daughter. It was great. If only I could be pregnant all the time. But life didn't miraculously get better just because I had a baby or because I was getting along with my mother for once. It actually got worse. My drug use increased, and I continued to live in a pit of mire, all because I loathed myself to the ends of the earth. I kept putting myself in situations I thought I deserved.

I repeated my mother's history by leaving my daughter with my grandparents. I chose to live on the streets of downtown Ottawa and struggle each and every day to survive, rather than living with them and my adorable daughter.

By the time I reached twenty-two I had pushed my luck way too far with the courts. On February 6, 2001, when I walked into the courtroom for seemingly the hundredth time, I was handed a two-year sentence in a federal penitentiary, for numerous counts of theft, fraud, forgery, and possession of stolen property.

I had expected to get sixteen to eighteen months, to be served in the same institutions I had become familiar with over the past few years: the Ottawa Carleton Detention Centre, the Vanier Centre for Women in Brampton, or even the Quinte Detention Centre in Napanee. These were places where I had served large amounts of time, places where I knew the rules and the lay of the land. There would have been no surprises regarding what I would face or what was expected of me there. But the federal pen was something serious. So off to prison in Grand Valley I went, like a little kid scared of the dark.

If anything, adult prison made me a worse person, though mostly because of my own attitude. There was nothing they could tell me. I thought I knew it all. I just wanted to do my time and get back out on the street. I wasted my time getting caught up in the trouble that was going on and causing trouble where there was none. I told lies to the other inmates, trying to make myself out to be something bigger then I really was, and I promised people things that there was no chance I could deliver on.

I hung out with what I considered to be the cool group, and with this came the expectation to perform at a certain level, a level I knew nothing about. So I just did everything I was told to do. I guess I was the gopher. I would hold the drugs for the other girls so they wouldn't get in trouble. I would keep watch for the girls when they were doing something they weren't supposed to be doing. All just to be called "cool." We cool girls didn't do programs, or try to better our lives, because there was nothing wrong with us – it was the system that was screwed up. So I stayed until my statutory release date, or two-thirds of my sentence, which was about sixteen months.

When I walked out of Grand Valley, on November 29, 2002, I was far from ready to change my life. For the next four years I was stuck in a downward cycle of perpetual self-destruction. I was in and out of jail six or seven times for the same crimes: fraud, theft, possession; always something to make money to feed my out-of-control drug habit. I would get out of jail, do well for a short while, then end up right back in hell, sometimes in the very cell I'd just been released from. Every time I went back, it was as if I had never left.

Even though Pembroke is a small town, it is large enough to get away from people who are not good for you. I, however, was attracted to the bad crowd like metal to a magnet. If there was trouble to be found, you could always find me in the middle of it.

Everything I swore I would never do, I did. I went from a pot smoker and light drinker to an acid-dropping alcoholic to an occasional thief to a frequent fraud artist. Then I went from crack-smoking thief and fraud artist to a needle-using prostitute who would steal your toupée if it wasn't glued on tight. Each and every time I went back out there using, it knocked me down to a lower low.

I remember being raped by a john at gunpoint and being scared for my life, only to get away and rob the next john for every dime he had in his pocket. If I wasn't high, I couldn't stand existing.

Don't get me wrong, though. I loved my daughter and my grandparents with every ounce of love that was in me. They were the only reasons I didn't check out of this life. Every time I thought of ending it, and saving myself the torture of existing one more day, I thought of them and couldn't do it. I couldn't do that to them on top of everything I had already put them through. My family suffered the most throughout my addiction, I think because they were the people closest to me and because they cared for me.

But I was on a mission to make everyone hate me as much as I hated myself. They suffered theft of alcohol, money, credit cards, cheques, jewellery, cars, identification, antiques, and collectibles at my hands, just to name a few things. But no matter what I did, my grandparents still loved me, which at the time made me angrier than anything else. They weren't the only family victims of my insanity. I robbed my uncle and his wife of almost everything in their home and my mother and stepfather of large amounts of cash.

I have even robbed my own daughter. Not financially, but emotionally, a much deeper scar. My daughter has had to watch me come in and out of her life for the past nine years: there one minute; gone the next. She has watched the police take me away at least three times that I can recall, and is quite aware at this point that her mother is in prison for breaking the law and that her mother has a drug addiction problem. You would think she would hate me, but through the grace of God, she loves me, misses me, and looks forward to a future where Mommy is no longer sick.

So at the ripe old age of twenty-six I walked back through the doors of Grand Valley Institution for Women. It was the second federal sentence of my young life. For the same charges as ever but this time for three years. I entered the prison a broken woman with not a hope left in any part of me. I had no hope that I could or would ever change, that I could or would ever be a good mother to my daughter, that I could or would ever be a decent human being.

There must have been free cake to get me there, but one Sunday in March 2006 I found myself at one of the evening church services. A gentleman by the name of Carl, an ex-offender, was leading the service. I had heard many stories from born-again ex-cons and I thought they were all full of it. There was something different about this guy, though. He had been where I was, he had felt what I was feeling, and he had been just a hopeless as I was at that moment, yet there he was, a new creation. It made me ask, "What do I have to lose?"

I left that service that night with an ache in my heart that I couldn't explain. It wasn't the empty feeling I usually had but something different, something demanding to be noticed. I went back to my unit, closed my door behind me, and was overcome with a flood of emotion. The feeling was stronger than the thrill I had felt when I first tried drugs, and stronger than the feeling of joy I had when I returned to my mother after running away the first time. I dropped to my knees that night and begged God to take my life, such as it was, and do something with it.

That wasn't so long ago, and I'm just beginning to feel and understand the changes that have come over me. But since that moment, my life has changed in ways that I can't even put into words. But I'll do my best. For the first time in my life, I feel a sense of peace in my heart, and I know that the void I had been trying to fill for so many years – with drugs, with attempts to gain my mother's love – is finally being filled. Not with anything manmade, or earthbound, but with the love and grace of my Lord. This love is unconditional and enduring, whereas the love I had been striving for was anything but.

I have finally been able to let go of some of the anger I carried around for so long, and that has left room for other human emotions to come through. And boy, have they ever come through. I even find myself crying during Charmin toilet paper commercials. Once I let go of the anger I was able to let go of my feelings of abandonment and resentment. I realized that all those years I was alone and unwanted, I never really was: God was always there for me, which is probably why I am still here to talk about it. I am now able to quit blaming others for my bad choices, and, at the same time, to quit feeling to blame for the way others treated me.

I used to look in the mirror and loathe everything about myself. Now I *love* everything about myself. I know I am a child of God, that I am lovable and capable. Recently I read these words, from Psalm 40:2: "God lifted me out of the mud and mire and placed my feet on a rock so that I would have a solid place to stand." That is exactly what God has done for me. He continues each and every day to do great things in my life. I have been able to stop doing things that were unhealthy for me and to separate myself from the people who are not healthy for me. He has helped me to stop being judgmental toward others and has given me the ability to take a look at myself through his own loving eyes. He is giving me the opportunity to grow more in him each day.

I no longer want the life I used to live. I no longer want to be that person, and I don't have to be. God promises me, in 2 Corinthians 5:17, that "if any man be in Christ, he is a new creature: old things are passed away; behold, all things are become new."

I hold on to that promise every day. My past does not define who I am today. It only defines what I am capable of withstanding, and what I am capable of helping others to defeat. I have the grace of God in my life. There is nothing I can't do with the strength of my Lord Jesus Christ.

CONCLUSION

Eleanor Clitheroe

I trust that the stories in this book have created some doubt in your mind about a widely held view of offenders: that they plan their crimes rationally, execute them calculatingly, resist justice for them energetically, and decline to try to rise above their actions and live a better life.

It's no surprise that many of us believe this. The recidivism rate of prisoners justifies our doubts that ex-offenders can be successfully reintegrated into their homes and our neighbourhoods. It's only natural that we try to protect ourselves by throwing up barriers to their restoration.

But it doesn't take much to demythologize this

view. The fact is, most criminals are more like the women whose stories you have read here than like the hard cases featured on *Law and Order* and a myriad of other television crime shows. For every female sociopath in prison there are dozens and dozens of Deweys and Viviennes and Stephanies – women whose personal and economic circumstances drew them into criminal acts.

Understanding the role that circumstances play in these situations is not to say that people have no free will – that they are determined by their situations to commit crime. We have seen in this book that ex-offenders, with the help of their families and communities, can choose to leave crime behind them, and can succeed in doing so. If choice has something to do with leaving crime behind, it must also have something to do with the commission of crime in the first place. But the key to this truth is in the phrase "with the help of their families and communities." As you have seen in this book, when ex-offenders are lent a helping hand by individuals and groups, they can and do break free from their past and build a better future, both for themselves and their loved ones.

It took me a while to shake free of this myth about ex-offenders myself. I have always been a church-goer and have supported social justice causes, but until recently I gave little thought to the plight of prisoners and their families. After working in government I had risen to the top of Ontario's Hydro One, becoming its CEO. Anyone who knows anything about corporate life knows that corporations virtually own their workers. Life at the top can be very exciting, occupying every waking thought and sleeping dream. However, as I found out, mother corporation not only can take you places you never imagined, but she can also cannibalize you.

So how, then, did I get from there to here, minis-tering in an Anglican parish and directing Prison Fellowship Canada? Many have asked me this ques-tion. I will answer it in the briefest possible way insofar as it shows how the scales fell from my eyes so I could see the reality of prisoners and their families in this country.

On July 19, 2002, I was fired, in a very public way, from my job as CEO of Hydro One, for alleged financial improprieties. The innuendo and media commentary ruined my reputation and my career. I became a "public figure" and my family and I lost our privacy. Friends, acquaintances, and business colleagues shunned me. I lost much of what I had built up over the preceding thirty years, including my career, income, pension and financial security, house, hobbies, network of business acquaintances, reputation, community, identity, and self-respect. I had little left but the support of my immediate family and close friends, and my faith in God.

This led me to enter seminary training at Wycliffe College in the University of Toronto. I had been a churchgoer from my youth and had always entertained thoughts of doing this – though I imagined it as an interesting retirement project. But somehow, through the grace of God, my own social downfall moved me into training that has led to my present ministry.

Naturally, my troubles do not compare with the troubles experienced by those caught up in the criminal-justice system. When I felt marginalized and helpless, I had the resources to reconnect with society. Others are not nearly so lucky. For the women you have read about in this book, a severe lack of support in their lives pushed them toward crime. My experience did, however, serve to awaken me to the plight of the disadvantaged. Like the other women in this book, I was able to rebuild my life only through faith in God and the firm support of a loving community.

As a result of all this, I am better able to sense the frustration many feel when confronted with criminals and their place in society. That frustration is caused by the conflict between two streams of thought about justice in the face of the reality of crime that have developed over the centuries, both of them flowing from religious beliefs.

One stream of thought holds that criminals deserve to be punished and that punishment will cause them to reform. Restraining them, constraining them, and even, in the case of capital punishment, terminating them are believed to have the potential to save their souls.

This is called punitive or retributive justice. This view also includes the idea that vengeance is a corrective measure for the victim and society. Balancing the scales by inflicting the appropriate amount of damage on the offender is thought to remedy, to the extent possible, the injustice done to the victim and the community. It is also thought to protect the community by deterring the offenders or potential offenders from future crime.

The other stream of thought, called restorative justice, acknowledges that broken relationships, particularly those caused by crime, have a severe impact not only on the offender and victims, but also on the victims' circle of family and friends, the offenders' family and friends, especially their children, and the communities within which all of these people live. Those who hold this view reject retribution for its inability to make individuals and communities whole.

Restorative justice is viewed as possible only through compassion, mercy, forgiveness, and integration, to the extent feasible, of all affected by the crime through an often painful process of healing and reintegration into community. While difficult, this approach concludes that restoration to mental, physical, emotional, and spiritual wholeness of individuals and society is only possible when everyone is engaged in the effort to repair the broken relationships and damage.

In restorative justice, the offender is not the only focus of justice. The restoration of the victim and the community are balanced with the restoration of the offender, not out of pity for the offender, but in the realization that reparation of damage and forward movement toward wholeness cannot be achieved by focusing on one affected party alone.

The voices of the women in this book speak loud and clear of the need for restorative justice, and I thank them for sharing their stories with us.

∞

There is significant biblical support for the proposition that God's justice is founded not on punishment, vengeance, and retribution but on compassion, mercy, reconciliation, and forgiveness. A restorative and healing understanding of God's justice has implications for how we undertake the restoration of those whose lives are broken by crime.

Space does not allow for a full discussion of the prophetic role of Jesus and its link to the theme of restorative justice that runs like a golden thread through the Old Testament – particularly in the writings of the prophets – and on into the New Testament. Instead, let's take a brief look at one Gospel text that shows God's justice to be restorative, not punitive. I'm speaking of the story of the woman caught in adultery, as found in John 8:1-11.

The tendency, in reading this passage, is to focus on the woman and the varying approaches to judgment shown by the Pharisees and Jesus. But in fact this is the inner story that's part of a bigger story: an argument between Jesus and the Pharisees regarding the validity of Jesus' teachings on God's justice.

The story immediately preceding this one is an exchange between the chief priests and Pharisees of the Sanhedrin, on the one hand, and Nicodemus, also a Pharisee and a member of the Sanhedrin, on the other. It concludes with the view that Jesus did not have a prophetic voice and so could not claim to stand in the tradition of the prophets on matters of justice. John 7:52 quotes the majority position of the Pharisees – that a prophet does not come out of Galilee. Which, of course, is where Jesus had been living and teaching.

The text in John 8 does not tell us about the background of the unnamed adulterous woman, but the story does tell us about the oppression and marginalization that surrounded women, and this woman in particular, in Jesus' time. The woman is brought unnecessarily out into the temple court for this debate. In a way a crime was being perpetrated against her as the debaters treated her as a prop for their argument.

The woman's male counterpart is nowhere in evidence and does not seem to be accused. This in spite of the fact that the law (see Deuteronomy 22:22 and Leviticus 20:10) required the punishment of both parties caught in adultery. It was required that the offenders to be "caught in the act," so it is clear that the woman's companion was known. While the woman may have broken the law, justice was not being impartially meted out. All the parties to the crime are not being engaged with the determination of justice in mind.

All the parties? you may ask. It is not known how many others were engaged in the crime. Had she been beaten by her husband, driven out to find solace with someone else? Was she poor and seeking to feed herself and her children through prostitution? Was she marginalized by her community? Was she a young girl in love with an older and more authoritative man? Was her own husband unfaithful?

The woman was an Israelite, part of a subjugated people under Rome and very likely poor. None of these circumstances that bring other people into the complex issues surrounding the commission of a crime seem to be up for consideration. She, alone, is standing under judgment.

The woman's age and experience are not considered. She is possibly quite young, perhapes a betrothed virgin (Deuteronomy 22: 23-24). She may be young girl, a child, for whom no regard other than as a piece of property is afforded. Roman law did not permit Israelites to carry out the death sentence. The abuse of this young girl and her possible execution was not for the purpose of delivering justice but of trapping Jesus into condoning an act against the Empire.

What does Jesus do? He writes with his finger in the dust. This is in stark contrast to the stone tablets of the law written by God for Moses. His answer includes the community in the crime of the woman. There does not seem to be any question that the woman broke the law. The question is what to do about it. Jesus suggests that each person reflecting on what God's justice is for the woman reflect on their own role in the crime. Only the person who has no role in the crime – who is without sin in their lives and in the community – can demand punishment, that is, cast the first stone.

This is now what was expected. Deuteronomy 17:7 requires witnesses to the act to be the first to throw stones at the condemned person. The witnesses would be some of the most offended parties in the community, actually having seen the offence occur, and would also constitute direct, rather than circumstantial evidence, of the crime. Jesus does not overturn the law; he simply asks that only those who are without sin assume the role of the victim and cast the first stone. The response of the assembled lawgivers is that none of them can honestly disconnect themselves from the crime of this woman. Crime is not an isolated event. It engages the whole community and each individual in it. Her crime is a reflection on them.

Jesus then addresses the woman. He does not condone her actions, but he does not cease to treat her with human dignity and respect. He straightens up when he speaks to her and looks at her. He restores her self-worth. In so doing, he has enabled her to go forward and tells her that she can now live in a transformed way, leaving her brokenness and life of sin behind. It is unlikely that her society would accept her as she had been before the adultery, but he tells her that she is able to make choices in how to live her life, not under the influence of others, but in her human and God-given dignity.

The story of this woman reflects the very essence of restorative justice. The entire community is involved in the causes of and brokenness resulting from crime and must take up responsibility. It is not by punishment and death that humans are transformed, that communities are strengthened, and that victims are freed from brokenness. Rather, they are transformed by the restoration of self-worth to the offender, the acknowledgment of responsibility by the community, and the freedom from brokenness of the victim through the transformation of both offender and community.

And here's the main point. Jesus affirms the

prophets' call to set prisoners free from the barriers that prevent them from belonging to the community. He also affirms the prophets' condemnation of leaders who do not make efforts to form a society in which communities, victims, and offenders can be restored to wholeness.

There is an open-ended reality to Jesus' mission here on earth. It is to continue through his disciples and through his church. You – we – are Jesus in the here and now. Our actions in taking responsibility for those who cannot look after themselves will bring, step by step, the kingdom into being. It is not just Jesus who is to heal the sick, feed the hungry, look after the poor, clothe the naked, and bring back those who have strayed. It is also we his disciples who are to do this.

It is interesting how Jesus always sends the people he helps back into their communities. There isn't a doubt in my mind, or in the minds of the women who have shared their stories with you in this book, that restoration, both personal and social, begins with this gracious command, this gracious invitation, to rise.

PRISON
FELLOWSHIP
CANADA

PRISON FELLOWSHIP CANADA (PFC) is a not-for-profit Christian organization and a chartered member of Prison Fellowship International (PFI). Prison Fellowship Canada, a prayer-based Christian ministry, is dedicated to meeting the needs of those affected by crime, through churches, local chapters, and prayer partners across the country.

PFC volunteers bring fellowship and support to prisoners and young offenders through in-prison Bible studies, chapel services, one-to-one mentoring, discipleship, and pre-release training. In 2007, PFC is piloting a few aftercare programmes with churches in Ottawa and Winnipeg. This year will also see the pilot of Sycamore Tree, a programme that brings offenders and victims together in a series of healing and transforming sessions.

For the families of inmates and ex-offenders, Angel Tree provides three programmes:

- **Angel Tree Christmas**, where the child of an inmate or ex-offender is given a gift in their parent's name. Volunteers purchase, wrap, and deliver the gifts, hoping to establish a link between the families and the local churches.

- **Angel Tree Camping** sends children of offenders to wonderful Christian camps across Canada in their parent's name. This experience can be life changing in so many ways.

- **Angel Tree *In the Loop*** provides a programme for teens at risk. The programme will offer leadership training, camping, and job experiences, all under the mentorship of a Christian volunteer.

To volunteer or for more information please e-mail Prison Fellowship Canada at info@prisonfellowship.ca, or call 1.888.470.2748 or (416) 848.4793.